Contents

(Since some items inevitably appear in many photographs, this listing should be read only as a guide to the main items to be found in each chapter or to their first appearance; only certain major items are listed more than once to draw the reader's attention to useful photographs in more than one chapter. Listings within each chapter are not in order of appearance but in logical groupings: uniforms generally precede equipment and weapons.)

Introduction

The evolution of the GI's uniforms during World War II has had a profound effect upon many armies throughout the world since 1945. The United States Army was the first to apply itself to designing a system of military combat clothing that would be comfortable, hard-wearing, and suitable to the needs of the soldier in all the different climatic regions in which he might be called upon to fight. Until 1941 the major military powers equipped their soldiers with a basic service uniform in which they had to fight, drill on the parade ground, and travel home on furlough. Even what was in many respects the best equipped army of the day - the German Wehrmacht - sent its divisions into battle in closed-collar tunics embellished with braid, metal badges and decorations; and committed them to the arctic conditions of their first winter on the Russian steppes wearing basically the same uniforms that they had worn during their triumphant progress across Europe in summer 1940.

The result of the US efforts was the "layering" system: the production of combat clothing for use in temperate zones which, with the addition of extra layers, would be suitable in colder temperatures. Probably the classic example of this is the M1943 field jacket; it is no exaggeration to say that this garment was the forerunner of virtually all the combat jackets used by the world's armies since 1945. Materials have changed, detail has been improved; but the four-pocket, thigh-length, windproof and water-resistant jacket remains the basic garment of the modern fighting man.

This book is intended to give anyone with an interest in the period 1941-45 a clear visual idea of what the United States Army combat soldier wore and carried. This is, to our knowledge, the first time that an attempt has been made, using the "re-enactment" technique, to show actual contemporary uniforms and equipment being worn in as near to realistic settings as is practically possible. (We would emphasise that the members of the 29th Historical Association and the other models appearing on these pages agreed to simulate battlefront poses purely for the sake of a degree of visual realism, and in a proper spirit of respect for the soldiers who wore these uniforms in earnest.)

The use of color throughout the book also gives the reader the opportunity to appreciate the wide range of differing shades of "olive drab" produced during the war, a luxury denied by the oft-reproduced black and white photographs of the 1940s. We hope that this color reference will prove useful to a wide readership encompassing modellers, militaria collectors, studio wardrobe and prop departments, illustrators and many others. While official shade numbers of olive drab are quoted in many of our captions, it should be noted that contemporary Army regulations and specifications often omitted them, limiting detail to such nowadays less than helpful phrases as "light shade" or "dark shade". It was not until the regulation AR 600-35 of 31 March 1944 that numbered shades were specified for officers' uniform items; we quote these retrospectively in appropriate captions, but the inevitable variations due to purchase from different manufacturers, and age, should be borne in mind.

For practical reasons we have confined our study to the "average" GI (as if there were such a man) and company officer of some of the main combat branches of the US Army. We have not set out to catalogue every possible item of US military gear; for those who require such information there are other books available which are organised to offer classification and specification data in greater depth of detail. In order to include as many photographs reproduced to as large a size as possible in the available space, we have limited most captions to basic identification data, while including a little basic background on non-conventional infantry organisations such as the Airborne, Rangers, and 1st Special Service Force.

Readers should note that where possible the descriptive terms which we use for garments are those found on the labels of contemporary items or in World War II Quartermaster catalogues - though at times even these can be contradictory. All dates quoted (in parentheses) from particular illustrated items of clothing are the pattern date, not the date of manufacture. All items photographed here are, to the best of our knowledge, of original wartime manufacture; and are assembled here in combinations confirmed by wartime photographs. In the relatively few cases where we have added formation insignia, there is photographic evidence for that combination of gear being worn and carried by that formation.

We had an immense amount of fun producing this book, and in the process met a lot of very helpful people. We hope the result will give as much pleasure to our readers.

R.G.W.
Finglesham, Kent
June 1993

THE WORLD WAR II GI

US Army Uniforms 1941–45
in Color Photographs

RICHARD WINDROW AND TIM HAWKINS

THE CROWOOD PRESS

First published in 1993 by Windrow & Greene

Paperback edition
published in 2008 by
The Crowood Press Ltd
Ramsbury, Marlborough
Wiltshire SN8 2HR

www.crowood.com

British Library Cataloguing-in-Publication Data
A catalogue record for this book is available from the
British Library.

ISBN 978 1 84797 033 6

Designed by John Anastasio/Creative Line

Printed in Singapore by Craft Print International Ltd

The US Soldier, 1941-42

(Above) Two US infantrymen in field uniforms and gear demonstrating the slight differences typical of the months before and after Pearl Harbor.

On the right, a pre-December 1941 GI wears the enlisted man's (hereafter, EM's) M1939 olive drab (hereafter, OD) wool four-pocket service coat, with OD wool shirt and black tie, M1937 light shade OD wool trousers, M1938 canvas leggings and service shoes. His webbing gear comprises the M1918 cartridge belt and M1910 haversack. He has an M1917 helmet with a leather chinstrap, and a service gasmask; and is armed with an M1903 .30 cal. Springfield bolt action rifle with an M1907 leather sling.

The left hand man wears gear more typical of the early months of 1942, particularly the "Parsons" OD field jacket, second pattern (dated 6 May 1941), in place of the wool service coat. His webbing is the M1923 dismounted cartridge belt and an M1928 haversack. The helmet is the M1917A1 with web chin-strap; and his Springfield rifle has a modified buttstock.

(Left) Side views of the two Pearl Harbor period infantrymen. The GI on the right has an M1905 bayonet in an early leather scabbard. He wears the M1910 haversack in marching order, with the M1910 pack carrier fitted to the bottom containing his blanket roll. The left hand soldier has the M1928 haversack with meat can pouch. At his right hip he carries an M1910 canteen. The modified butt of his Springfield rifle is obvious in profile; this is the 1931 pistol grip model, contrasting with the straight butt model on the right. Both men have the M1910 T-handle entrenching tool strapped to their packs.

(Left) Basic enlisted men's service uniform worn in two slightly different configurations on the perimeter of a US Army base, Zone of the Interior, 1942. Both GIs wear the M1939 wool serge 18oz OD service coat, light shade OD wool trousers loose over russet leather service shoes, OD wool shirt, and mohair necktie. (This latter was experimentally introduced in light OD shade 3 in 1941-42; became standard in September 1942; and was replaced for all uniforms by one in khaki shade 5 from September 1943, though this was seen with wool uniforms before that date.)

The left hand man wears the EM's OD wool serge service cap with russet leather visor and chinstrap, and brass US Army cap badge in disc form. The EM's russet leather garrison belt was discontinued during 1942. For sentry duty the soldier on the right wears an M1936 pistol belt with a shotshell pouch for his Winchester 12-gauge shotgun Model 1897, a riot type pump-action five-shot weapon originally issued in WWI for close-quarter trench fighting. Despite the date the M1917 helmet was still issued to troops in the ZI.

(Below left) Detail of the shotshell pouch, holding 12 rounds.

(Right) The M1910 haversack, marching order, with the pack carrier attached. This archaic design accomodated only a restricted list of items, taking little account of the needs of the soldier in the field. Rations and toilet items were carried in the haversack; the mess tins ("meat cans") in the detachable outer pouch; blanket, shelter half and minimal extra clothing in a vertical roll in the lower pack carrier; bayonet, entrenching tool and rolled overcoat could be attached to the outside. Its integral suspenders attached directly to the cartridge belt. Note button closure of the meat can pouch; the modified M1928 pack had the pouch fastened with a buckled strap. The bayonet is an M1905 in an early leather scabbard.

(Right) Sergeant and private of infantry wearing summer/ tropical uniforms in the Panama Canal Zone, 1941. Both men wear the khaki cotton shirt and trousers, shade 1, sometimes referred to as "chinos". The sentry has an M1917A1 helmet, M1923 cartridge belt, M1903 Springfield with long M1905 bayonet and M1910 scabbard, and the service gasmask. The sergeant is wearing the EM's khaki cotton service cap, shirt with khaki mohair tie, and trousers loose over service shoes. Note that the shirts have a "convertible" collar, for smartness when worn open, or closed with a tie.

(Below) The M1938 EM's rubberized raincoat, this example dated 23 December 1940.

(Below right) The M1938 dismounted leggings, first pattern. Worn with the service shoe, these were made from canvas duck material and just over 12ins. high. They were unpopular with the troops, as they absorbed water, chafed the legs, and took too long to put on or take off - which could also cause painful delays when treating foot or leg injuries.

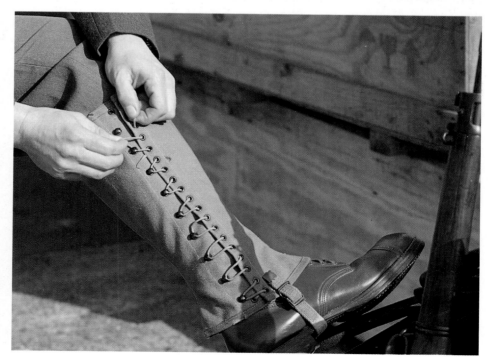

(**Left**) *Trooper and officer of cavalry, Zone of the Interior, 1942. The trooper, on the left, wears an M1911 service hat in "beaver color" felt with yellow cavalry cords, OD coat-style wool shirt, and wool elastique breeches. He has an M1918 mounted cartridge belt, M1907 suspenders, and an M1911A1 .45 pistol in an M1912 mounted holster. The major, right, wears officer's summer shirt and breeches in khaki cotton. His service hat differs only in having officer's cords of interwoven black and gold; he wears a russet M1921 "Sam Browne" belt (discontinued in June 1943). Note the gold-colored oakleaf rank insignia on the right point of his shirt collar; branch of service insignia were pinned to the left point.*

(**Above**) *The two cavalrymen wear legging top laced boots of elk leather, common to all ranks. Note the M1918 double-pouch pistol magazine pocket on the trooper's M1918 mounted belt, which lacked one rifle ammunition pocket at front* left to accomodate it, and his M1907 suspenders. He wears no national or branch collar insignia on his shirt; enlisted men discontinued this practice during the war, to save on wear and tear to the shirts.

(**Left**) *Detail of the elk hide legging top laced riding boots of the US Cavalry. Note that the illustrated breeches are private purchase; the legs are secured with buttons rather than the laces found on issue breeches.*

(Below) A GI wearing the first pattern "Parsons" OD field jacket. The specification for this famous jacket - the first ever designed specifically for combat, in an age when other armies still used wool service tunics or blouses for parade and battlefield alike - was laid down by General Parsons, commander of the US Army III Corps, in early 1940. The intention was to replace the four-pocket wool service coat for field service with a comfortable, loose-fitting jacket resembling a civilian windcheater. The first specification number issued by the Philadelphia Quartermaster Depot, in October 1940, was PQD No.20. The "olive drab field jacket" was described as a cotton-shelled windproof jacket with flannel lining. It had two diagonal front pockets fitted with button-down flaps, an integral rear half-belt, two tightening tabs at the hip fastening to a pair of buttons on the rear skirt, and buttoned tightening tabs at each wrist. It had two lapels, a collar that could be worn up or down, and a zip up the front concealed by a flap fastened with six plastic buttons. This version of the field jacket is often called the "M38" by collectors, but there was no such contemporary designation.

Note also the M1941 mounted canteen cover and hanger which this GI holds.

(Above) Detail of the M1907 suspenders. Lacking the attachments for a haversack, these were retained solely by the cavalry at this late date, since the troopers had no need for a back-pack. The large brass rivet which allowed the M1912 mounted holster to pivot freely with the thigh movement of a rider is also visible. The riding gloves are private purchase items.

Service Uniforms, 1942–45

(Right) A GI newly arrived in England wears his M1939 EM's four-pocket wool service coat with brass buttons, wool trousers in OD shade 54, and russet leather service shoes. The coat had a "bi-swing" back (approved in November 1939 and discontinued from July 1942); it also had an integral cloth half-belt sewn in the back. Insignia are limited to his "collar brass": discs bearing, on the right collar, the US cypher, and on the left his branch of service device. The absence of any shoulder sleeve insignia is normal for a newly arrived soldier not yet assigned to a formation. He wears the EM's OD wool shirt, and the khaki mohair necktie standardised for all uniforms from September 1943. His OD wool serge garrison cap replaced the visored service cap for overseas wear (and increasingly in the ZI after 1941, when the latter was made a "limited standard" item). Early production caps had rounded crown corners and a top gusset; for ease of manufacture the corners were squared and the gusset disappeared from later production models. The pale blue corded piping round the top edges of the curtain indicates the infantry; later caps are often found without branch of service piping. Over his shoulder he carries the service gasmask in its bulky case.

(Below) Two infantry NCOs relax to some light music. The staff sergeant, right, wears standard service shoes with toecap, a half rubber "tap" on the sole, leather instep and rubber heels. His light shade OD wool trousers are dated 9 November 1937. The "bi-swing" pleat of his jacket is just visible behind his left shoulder. The technician/grade 3, left, wears dark OD shade 33 18oz wool trousers (dated April 1944); and the later simplified service shoe with no toecaps and one-piece rubber sole. Note the EM's coat style wool shirt, khaki mohair tie and tan socks.

(**Left**) *Walking out in shirtsleeves, this infantryman wears the EM's wool shirt with khaki mohair tie, wool trousers and service shoes. His garrison cap is the later pattern with squared corners and no crown gusset, but has infantry piping. On the left shoulder of his shirt (and that of the service coat, dated 10 July 1942, carried over his arm) can be seen the blue and gray SSI of the 29th Infantry Division. When the 29th formed in WWI it was raised from the Maryland/ Pennsylvania border; as this region had supplied troops to both sides in the Civil War it was known as the "Blue & Gray Division", and used these colors in the Asian "yin and yang" good luck symbol of the divisional shoulder patch.*

(**Below left**) *OD coat style flannel shirt, khaki mohair tie, and dark shade OD 33 wool trousers supported by the webbing M1937 waist belt with the EM's open-frame black metal buckle. Note that this shirt is a later style to that above; it has a convertible collar and no front placket.*

(**Below right**) *Back pocket detail of a pair of EM's light OD wool trousers. These were issued with no flaps on the hip pockets, but GIs often added a flap or a button to one pocket for security.*

(**Right**) *Late summer 1944: a technician/grade 3 paratrooper of the 101st Airborne Division, on leave after the Normandy campaign and fraternising with the locals, shows off the range of insignia which could appear on the wool service coat. His dark shade 33 wool trousers are bloused over the Corcoran jump boots which mark his elite Airborne status. His early pattern garrison cap bears the Glider/Airborne badge.*

His collar points display the US cypher and infantry crossed muskets on EM's brass discs. His parachutist's qualification badge ("jumpwings") is worn above his left breast pocket; on the pocket flap is the blue enamel and silver Combat Infantryman badge marking a combat veteran. On his left shoulder is the SSI of the 101st Airborne Division; his rank chevrons are worn on both upper arms. On his left forearm is the British-made 1944 Pathfinder's badge, a golden-yellow winged torch with red flames on a purple or dark blue field, issued square but usually trimmed to the edge of the device. Below this appear three overseas service "hash" marks, each indicating six months abroad (these would suggest that he has transferred to his present unit from the 82nd Airborne).

(**Left**) *Detail of the Glider/Airborne badge on an early style EM's wool garrison cap. The pale blue branch of service piping denotes infantry, as does the surround of the badge. From 1943 a common design for all Airborne troops was issued, replacing the different parachute, glider, infantry and artillery versions which had appeared since 1940; but the earlier versions, such as this intermediate combined parachute/glider device in infantry colors, would have been retained by veterans who had them. By tradition, a paratrooper kept a silver dollar sewn behind the cap badge, as an aid in a bar room brawl or to get him back to base when all else was spent.*

Insignia

Representative examples of the main categories of insignia worn on US Army service uniform. On combat uniforms practice varied widely: rank insignia was generally worn in the ETO and MTO, though often discreetly; the display, or not, of "patches" on field jackets varied from division to division.

Branch of service colors were displayed as piping on EM's garrison caps and cords on service hats; among the most common were light blue (infantry), yellow (cavalry), scarlet (artillery), green & white (armored), orange & white (signals), scarlet & white (engineers), maroon & white (medical). All officers' piping and cords were interwoven gold and black.

The US national coat of arms in yellow metal was worn on service caps, on a disc by EM *(1)* and in pierced form by officers (see p.17). Officers wore rank insignia on the left front of garrison caps; EM could wear enamelled unit crests in this position, though they were rarely seen overseas. Airborne troops' circular embroidered badges, e.g. the 1943 combined type *(2)*, were made "mirrored", as officers wore theirs on the right front of the cap.

On the right coat collar EM wore the "U.S." cypher on a 1in. yellow metal disc *(3)*. On the left collar they wore branch of service devices on discs, e.g.:*(4)* Signal Corps, *(5)* Military Police, *(6)* Armored Forces, *(7)* Artillery, *(8)* Corps of Engineers, *(9)* Infantry, etc. Officers wore pierced national cyphers *(10)* on both coat collar points, above branch devices on both lapels, e.g.:*(11)* Chemical Warfare Service, *(12)* Armored Infantry, *(13)* Signal Corps, *(14)* Artillery, *(15)* Corps of Engineers, *(16)* Infantry, etc. Officers wore one cypher and one branch device on their right and left shirt collar points respectively.

Officers' rank insignia were worn on the left front of the garrison cap, and on the coat epaulettes (generals alone wore rank stars on both shirt

collar points): e.g. *(17)* second lieutenant, *(18)* first lieutenant, *(19)* captain, *(20)* major.

NCOs' rank chevrons and "rockers" were worn on both upper arms of coats and shirts. Originally a distinction was drawn between insignia of OD felt sewn to a dark blue wool field (left in photo) for OD uniforms, and those embroidered in khaki on dark blue cotton (right in photo) for khaki uniforms; but the distinction broke down in practice: *(21)* master sergeant/1st grade, *(22)* staff sergeant/2nd grade, *(23)* corporal/5th grade, *(24)* first sergeant/2nd grade, *(25)* sergeant/4th grade, *(26)* technician/5th grade, *(27)* private first class. Diagonal stripes on the left forearm *(28)* marked completed three-year enlistments; above them, and far more common in WWII, were worn straight six-month overseas service stripes *(29)*.

On the left breast pocket flap were worn marksman's badges, here *(30)* basic, with hangers for rifle and machine gun, *(31)* expert, with hangers for pistol and carbine. The Combat Infantryman's badge *(32)* was worn on or above the flap, medal ribbons above it: e.g.*(33)* Purple Heart, *(34)* 1941 Army Good Conduct Medal, *(35)* Europe, Africa, Middle East Medal. The Presidential Unit Citation bar *(36)* was worn above the right breast pocket.

Shoulder sleeve insignia or "patches" were worn on the left shoulder of service coats, shirts, and sometimes field jackets. The following examples are all divisions unless otherwise captioned: *(37)* 10th Mtn., *(38)* 101st Abn., *(39)* 82nd Abn., *(40)* 3rd Inf., *(41)* 95th Inf., *(42)* 29th Inf., *(43)* 5th Army, *(44)* 104th Inf., *(45)* Ranger Battalions, *(46)* 35th Inf.,*(47)* 89th Inf., *(48)* 45th Inf., *(49)* 28th Inf., *(50)* 80th Inf., *(51)* 103rd Inf., *(52)* 9th Inf., *(53)* 4th Armd. - basic design common to all armd.divs.,*(54)* 4th Inf., *(55)* 30th Inf. - as intended, but actually worn horizontally, *(56)* 17th Abn., *(57)* 106th Inf.; and *(58)* official photographer's tab.

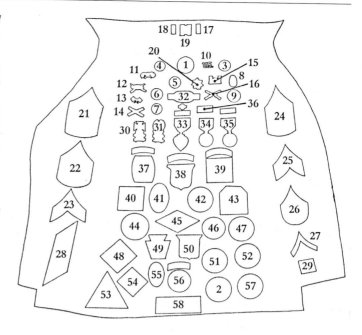

(Above) Looking for his billet, this GI wears the EM's OD roll collar wool melton overcoat issued in March 1940. It had eight large brass front buttons, the upper pair concealed under the deep lapels. He has the later style garrison cap; note branch piping style on right side.

(Top left) Note the detail differences between these two early examples of the EM's "field jacket, US Army, ETO." On the left is a British-made version (dated 1943), inspired by the British battledress blouse. He also has a British-made garrison cap, and dark OD 33 20oz wool trousers, a thicker material for cold climates. The jacket on the right is a US-made model (dated 1942), inspired by the Parsons OD field jacket; it has a double closure and a gas flap, and slash pockets with forward-buttoning flaps. This GI has a US-made cap; note that neither cap has curtain piping. The shoulder holster is the M7 model.

(Center) Rear view of the ETO jackets. Note their "bi-swing" backs, and the waistband fastening on the left hand jacket. The European Theatre of Operations jacket was born of a direct request from General Eisenhower to the Quartermaster Dept. for a jacket similar in design to the British battledress, that could be worn both in combat and as a dress tunic. A later model, of improved material and design, was generally issued in 1944, but saw little - if any - combat, as the GIs preferred to keep it for dress use. Upon return to the States the troops were entitled to wear it in place of the wool service coat.

(Below) Two later model "Ike" or OD wool field jackets; again, note detail differences. The GI on the left has one in dark OD shade 33 (dated 1944). The man on the right wears a cut-down four-pocket service coat; due to shortages of the issue version, GIs quite often had one tailored from a service coat.

Officers' Uniforms

(Right) The officer's service coat in wool elastique, in the dark OD shade 51 (dated 4 November 1942). At the rear are two pleats, some 3in. deep, running from the meeting of the shoulder seam and the armhole down to the waistline: the "bi-swing" back. There is a rear central vent from the waistline to the bottom edge of the skirt; and note the complete integral belt, identifying the model authorised in November 1942. The two lower pockets are internally hung. Commissioned rank was indicated on all officers' service coats by the half-inch strip of OD shade 53 mohair braid 3ins. above the cuffs. The collars bear cut-out "U.S." cyphers, the lapels the infantry branch's crossed muskets device; and the epaulettes the single silver rank bars of first lieutenant.

The jacket is worn here with a dark shade OD winter service shirt and khaki mohair tie. (Officers had the option of wearing wool shirts in either OD shade 50, dark shade 51, light shade 54, or khaki shade 1, or cotton shirts in khaki shade 1.) The officer's gold/black-piped garrison cap in OD shade 51, with rounded crown corners and top gusset, bears the rank bar at left front. His trousers (dated 19 March 1944) are of the optional light shade officially described as "drab", but popularly known as "pinks".

(Left) A captain of the 2nd Infantry Division wearing the officer's service cap of dark shade OD wool, with a band of lighter ribbed mohair braid, a russet leather visor and double chinstrap with leather slides, two small brass buttons bearing (like all brass US Army buttons) the national coat of arms; and the officers' pierced brass cap badge of the same device. He wears standard national, branch and rank insignia on the collar, lapels and epaulettes of his four-pocket service coat; and the large SSI of the 2nd Infantry Division sewn to the left shoulder. His shirt is the optional khaki cotton type.

(**Right**) Two infantry officers in shirtsleeves. The captain on the left wears the khaki cotton shirt and mohair tie with wool elastique dark OD trousers (dated 1942). On his right and left collar points are pinned his insignia of rank and branch respectively. (Crossed rifles first appeared on US infantry uniforms in 1875. Attempts to change the design to keep up with changing models of rifles were dropped in 1924, when this musket design was adopted.) His companion is wearing a dark OD officer's winter service shirt, khaki mohair tie, and officer's "pinks". Note that officers' shirts of all shades differed from those of enlisted men in having epaulettes. The M1937 web waist belts have the officer's style solid brass buckle plate.

(**Left**) 1944: somewhere in the South of England, our 2nd Infantry Division officers sample the delights of warm British beer. The varied appearance of officers' uniforms was due to their options over the choice of both shirt and trousers to wear with the dark OD service coat, and later the "Ike" jacket. The Officer's Guide suggested that each officer purchased at least two pairs of trousers. Dark shade OD were prescribed for use in the field, and were optional with the service coat; to avoid any unsightly difference of dark OD shades between coat and trousers purchased at different times or from different tailors, however, the other option - drab or "pink" wool elastique trousers - was recommended for at least one pair. For "arduous service" EM's OD trousers could also be bought, but were not to be worn with the dark OD officer's service coat.

(Right) 1944: an infantry officer asks directions of an MP in London. He wears an officer's quality ETO field jacket in dark OD shade 51 wool elastique, over a drab shirt, drab trousers and russet leather shoes. National, branch and rank insignia are worn on the "Ike" jacket exactly as on the four-pocket service coat. Over his arm he carries the second pattern of the officer's short overcoat, with a notched collar and no integral belt. Note the clothing bag at his feet.

The MP wears the EM's service coat and wool trousers in OD shade 54, M1938 leggings and service shoes. On duty outside a combat zone the "Snowdrop's" function is marked not only by a white-on-dark-blue "MP" brassard on his left arm, but by a white helmet liner with "MP" painted in black, white gloves, belt and leggings and whistle lanyard.

(Below left) A first lieutenant wearing the officer's short overcoat in its first pattern, with shawl collar and a buttoned integral belt.

Although it had been authorised since 1926, the March 1944 regulations retrospectively prescribed OD shade 52 for this coat. The only indications of rank were metal rank insignia pinned to the outer end of the epaulettes. This design was modified in 1943 when the belt was omitted and the shawl collar gave way to notched lapels. Note also the brown leather issue gloves.

(Below right) An officer's field overcoat (dated 17 December 1942). The front corners of the coat skirt could be buttoned back for ease of movement, and a tab on the reverse of the collar enabled it to be buttoned closed and upright. The coat came equipped with a button-in wool liner for the winter. Originally intended for issue to all ranks in place of the wool overcoat, this trench style coat was restricted to officers due to shortage of materials and time. There are slight differences between examples made in the USA and Britain, as with so many items subcontracted by the US Army for local manufacture.

Summer & Tropical Uniforms

(Right) On furlough in a Pacific theater rear area, 1945, these two GIs wear EM's "chino" shirt and trousers in khaki shade 1. The left hand man wears a second style khaki cotton garrison cap with pale blue infantry curtain piping; these were also made without piping. His EM's web waist belt is a 1in. wide WWI pattern, narrower than the M1937 which was 1³⁄₈in. or 2in. wide, with open frame black metal buckle. He wears service shoes; and 1944 Army issue sunglasses. The sergeant has a short-billed M1941 herringbone twill cap; and M1943 combat service boots - late in the war GIs often wore their chinos tucked into these combat boots even when off duty.

(Left) Two first lieutenants of infantry wearing summer tropical worsted (khaki gabardine) uniforms. The officer on the left wears a khaki garrison cap with gold/black cord piping; and a privately purchased khaki gabardine shirt, without shoulder straps, with the mohair tie. Note the brass buckle plate on his web trouser belt. His colleague wears the officer's summer service cap, summer service coat and trousers, described in the September 1942 regulations; this generally resembled the dark shade wool service coat, though with detachable buttons.

"You're In The Army Now..."

(Right) Second pattern HBT work suit. The left pocket is the same as on the first pattern. The right hand one now has a flap with a metal button. The lower pockets are patch style.

(Below) Lying under a jeep, a mechanic wears the first pattern OD one-piece herringbone twill (HBT) work suit. Adopted late in 1938, it was available in quantity in 1941. It had two patch pockets on the chest: the right hand one had a buttonless flap stitched down at either end; the left hand one, closed across the top, was open down the top half of the inside edge, to take watches, etc., and also had a stitched-in pencil holder. Note the mechanic's safety shoe resting on the fender; this had a composition sole and a steel box toecap.

(Above) Detail of ankle fastening on the one-piece herringbone twill suit, with adjustment tab and metal buttons.

(Right) Third pattern HBT work suits; the left hand example has metal buttons, the right has plastic. This third pattern has only one top pocket, with a buttoned flap.

(Below) In this line-up the left hand man has the first pattern HBT suit; only this pattern has an inner, buttoned pocket in the slash side pocket giving access to trousers worn under the suit. It has two patch rear pockets, a long wrench pocket on the right thigh, and a bi-swing back. The second man from the left has the second type suit, with a buttoned flap on the single right rear pocket, a bi-swing back and no wrench pocket. At right are two men in third-pattern suits; this has no bi-swing back, a wrench pocket, and no fastening to the flap on the rear pocket. The second and third patterns have a flap over the lower front patch pockets. All patterns have integral belts with tongueless metal buckles.

(Above left) Both these Signal Corps linemen wear the early pleated-pocket type of two-piece HBT work suit, also adopted in 1938 and issued during 1941. The GI up the pole has the M1941 HBT hat, based on the pre-war blue denim fatigue hat and popularly called the "Daisy Mae". The GI on the ground has the M1941 HBT fatigue cap, and carries an EE8B field telephone. Just visible are differences between the linemen's pouches: the pole man's is leather, modified with a clip on the flap and a hanger for tape on the bottom. The other, just visible under the GI's right arm, is canvas.

(Above right) Detail of second pattern M1938 dismounted leggings, with the number of eyelets reduced to eight, worn here with the lineman's climbing spurs.

(Right) Detail of the EE8B field telephone, in leather carrier.

(Left) An EE8B field telephone fitted in a wartime economy canvas carrier.

(Below) A GI works a portable field telephone exchange, as used in headquarters down to company level. He wears OD wool shirt and trousers, an M1941 knitted wool cap with the short visor turned up, and, around his neck, the speaker element of the telephone.

(Top right) The field telephone exchange, and a field desk and portable typewriter, also typical items for a tented company headquarters. Note K-ration dinner and supper units in color-printed packs.

(Bottom right) A folded shelter half, the cotton bag to hold eight wooden tent pins, one three-piece folding pole and a guy cord. Each GI would carry these items, joining them with those of a buddy to make up a two-man pup tent.

(*Above*) *Pouring water into a collapsible canvas bath, these GIs finish off their washday chores in camp. Drying on the pup tent can be seen both the white and olive drab cotton undershorts; to the right are a pair of OD wool socks, and the machine-knit long drawers; to the left, a pair of short winter drawers (both types adjusted at the back with a lace run through eyelets), and a sweatshirt. The crouching GI wears a long-sleeved, crew-necked white winter undershirt. On the tent in the background can be seen the OD version of the long drawers. The GI on the left wears the M1941 wool knit cap or "jeep cap"; issued in 1941 and intended* for wear under the M1 helmet in cold weather, it had a short stiffened visor, and the double-knit sides could be pulled down over the ears.

(*Left*) *The early Army poncho was made from OD rubberised cotton material (left); but wartime economies of strategic materials soon led to its production in synthetic resin-coated OD nylon fabric (right). Double snap fasteners on the edges allowed the forming of rudimentary sleeves, and metal grommets permitted ponchos to be tied together to make tent-like shelters. Neither type of poncho had a hood; both types had a drawstring neck closure.*

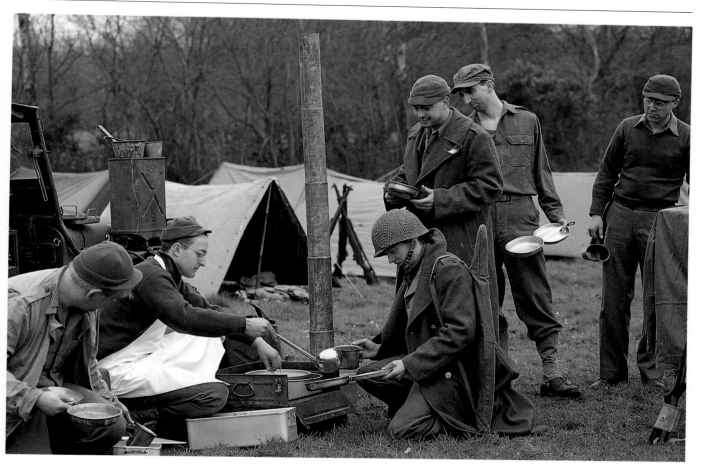

(Left) *Issuing K-rations, a cook hands out cartons with the breakfast meal on top. This consisted of canned meat and processed eggs, crackers, coffee, cereal and a fruit bar; there was also chewing gum, sugar and cigarettes. The GI on the right wears a V-neck sweater over a wool shirt and trousers. The cook has the five-button sweater with a low collar, and a cut-down pair of the M1938 leggings - GIs often did this for comfort. They both wear the M1941 wool knit cap - the comfortable but unsoldierly-looking headgear reputedly so hated by General Patton that he ordered a fine for any GI caught wearing one other than intended, i.e. under his M1 helmet. Note early M1938 EM's raincoat on the jeep's gas can.*

(Above) *Chow up...GIs line up by a small detachment cooking stove, the type used to feed from six to 30 men. Note the dippers on the inverted gas can on the wing of the jeep. The gas fed the burners on the stove via a rubber pipe. The man being served is wearing the EM's wool overcoat with brass buttons; slung over his shoulder is an M1 .30 cal. carbine in a canvas cover; in one hand he holds the two halves of his meat can set, in the other his canteen cup. The man behind him has an overcoat with OD plastic buttons (dated 21 November 1942). Note the spoon, carried at the ready in his lapel. The third man in line appears to have acquired an officer's flannel shirt with epaulettes. The GI kneeling at left is dipping coffee from a dixie.*

(Left) Detail of a supper carton from the K-rations; dinner and supper contents varied slightly, but each meal was supposed to include about 4oz. of meat (veal, spam, dried sausage, etc.), with cheese and crackers, and each day's meals included candy and gum, coffee, bouillon and other drink mixes, smokes and toilet paper. The three packs together were supposed to provide a daily intake of about 2830 calories. This is an early style carton, as issued from 1941, without color printing. Cartons issued from 1943 had a brown design for the breakfast ration, dark blue for dinner and dark green for supper.

(Center left) The stainless steel canteen cup into which the M1910 canteen fitted inside its canvas carrier; the folding handle is extended on the far side. Note the captured German Army issue combination fork and spoon set; members of the 29th Division thought them superior to the US issue "eating irons".

(Bottom left) These GIs have several versions of issue canteens to fill. At front left is the M1910 aluminium canteen and cap; behind it is an M1942 version with a black plastic cap. Center front is a blue enamelled version, only issued in 1942; center rear is a limited issue plastic canteen, only made in 1943, to save on aluminium. Right front is a M1942 aluminium version with a body seam and black plastic cap; right rear is the stainless steel version of the M1942. The canteen being filled is a black enamelled 1942 model; the issue of this type was not - as commonly supposed - limited to the US Marines in the Pacific theater.

Helmets

(Right) A classic shot of the M1 helmet, here with the painted insignia applied by men of the 29th Infantry Division. The painting of formation insignia on helmets was regulated, if at all, at unit and divisional level, but only a minority carried such decorations in the combat zone. The factory finish for helmets was a roughened, non-reflective OD paint.

Made from manganese steel and fitted with a separate inner liner, the M1 gave far superior protection to the dishpan-shaped M1917 helmet, which was still being produced as late as 1940 while the Ordnance Corps was looking for a suitable replacement. The liner of the M1 was initially made from compressed fibre, and was fitted with an adjustable suspension system of light cotton/rayon web straps to fit all sizes. The liner could be worn without the steel shell when in garrison or behind the lines, and had a narrow leather chinstrap to secure it when worn alone. The helmet shell had a webbing chinstrap, fixed to metal brackets under either side of the rim. It fastened under the chin with an interlocking metal fastener, but was rarely seen done up when in the front lines. When the helmet was worn complete the chinstrap of the liner was pulled up over the front rim of the helmet; the chinstrap of the steel shell was often fastened up over the rear rim.

(Left) Its two-piece design gave the M1 steel helmet many potential uses apart from being worn on the head. With the liner removed the steel shell could double as a washbasin, a cooking pot, an entrenching shovel, and, more often than not, as a hammer for driving in tent pins and stakes, as well as for more unsavoury purposes in cases of extreme emergency under heavy fire. This GI, using it for his morning ablutions in a sunny orchard, wears the OD sleeveless cotton summer undershirt and M1942 herringbone twill trousers. Note that the bracket under the far rim of the helmet shell is folded inward, which indicates that this is a late production model. On the first version these brackets were rigid, and thus prone to damage; the hinged-bracket type appeared before the end of the war.

(Above) The variations of the liner and suspension cradle found with the wartime M1 helmet. (Right) the first pattern fibre liner; (center) the first pattern plastic liner, retaining the same webbing cradle as the fibre liner; (top left) a fibre liner with the second pattern webbing; and (left foreground) the later plastic liner with second pattern webbing, a combination which remained unchanged until the 1960s.

(Left) The two types of liner for the M1 helmet. On the right is the early issue compressed fibre pattern covered with OD fabric. This is still quite often referred to as the "officer's" liner; in fact there was no difference between officers' and EM's liners. On the left is the later liner, of layered and bonded cloth and plastic construction; the difference in thickness between the two liners is plain. Note the eyelet at front center of the left hand liner, provided so that rank insignia could be fixed when worn alone behind the lines.

(Above) *A staff sergeant wears the M1 steel helmet with a US-made woven net, to which expedient foliage camouflage could be added to break up the outline of the helmet; the netting itself reduced the sheen of the metal, which could be a problem if it got wet or greasy. He wears the helmet chinstrap clipped round the back and the liner chinstrap over the front rim.*

(Above right) *A rear view of the same man. Visible on the back of his helmet, even through the netting, is the white-painted horizontal bar sometimes applied as a battlefield recognition aid to enable following troops to identify an NCO. Officers sometimes used a white vertical bar.*

(Below right) *An infantry officer in the ETO, 1944-45, wears a late pattern M1 helmet with hinged chinstrap brackets. The insignia of first lieutenant's rank is painted on the front, together with the "yin and yang" symbol of the 29th Infantry Division. Note also his GI issue spectacles, and the M3 6x30 binoculars.*

Boots

(Right) The russet leather service shoe - actually an ankle boot - with which the US Army entered the war. Made from fully chromed leather, they had toecaps, a rubber composition sole and heel, and were worn under the M1938 canvas leggings or, as here, as walking out shoes.

(Below) In 1943 the so-called "fleshout" service shoe was introduced, differing in being made with the rough, flesh side of the leather to the outside. If well packed with grease, boots made in this way give better protection against wet. To save leather they were made without toe caps; and they had full-length rubber soles instead of the previous partial "tap". Their official designation was shoes, service, reverse uppers, composition soles. They were for overseas use only.

(Above) At the same time as the reverse upper service shoe was introduced, the new M1943 combat service boot came under trial. Also made flesh side out and without toecaps, they did away with the necessity of wearing leggings by incorporating an integral 5in. deep leather cuff or gaiter fastened with two buckled straps. Although they were tested in North Africa in 1943, it was late 1944 before they were available in any numbers in the ETO.

(Top left) The distinctive high-laced parachute jumper boot, with its strong toecap and more substantial sole and heel, was designed to protect and support ankles and feet during the strains of a heavy landing. The leading edge of the heel was chamfered backwards to prevent snagging in the deploying parachute shroud lines. Usually referred to as "Corcorans", from the name of the original 1941 manufacturer, these jump boots were jealously sought after by non-parachute outfits, and just as jealously guarded by the paratroopers as a mark of their elite status. Permission to wear the highly shined jump boots with bloused trousers when in service uniform was a prized privilege.

(Left) The moulded rubber and canvas jungle boots, standardised in August 1942, lacked some of the sophisticated features of modern designs, but were much preferred by Pacific theater troops to the heavy service shoe and combat service boot. They had a full-length bellows tongue behind the front lacing.

(Top right) The initial design of these cloth-topped four-buckle overshoes, with rubber soles, was to protect the service shoes from extreme conditions. They replaced an early-war version with all-rubber uppers; and in 1945 were replaced in their turn by an overshoe with rubber uppers and five snap buckles.

(Above) The M1944 shoepac was first tested in Italy. A 12in. leather legging was fitted to a one-piece rubber sole and vamp with a waterproof seam; a steel shank was incorporated. Secured by laces through five pairs of holes on the foot and four pairs of hooks on the leg, these boots were intended for use in wet, muddy or snowy conditions. While much more waterproof than the M1943 combat boot they caused problems when worn for long periods. The troops' feet sweated excessively, and when they halted became painfully cold despite the felt inner sole and two pairs of wool socks.

Combat Dress: Pacific Theater

(Right) This GI wears an M1944 helmet net to keep out a variety of bloodsuckers; it fitted over the helmet and face and secured at the neck with a drawstring. The M1942 version of this net had no crown, merely tying round the helmet, and thus had only one stiffening rib in the net. He wears the M1942 one-piece jungle suit in camouflage herringbone twill material. When requested to provide jungle combat clothing in July 1942 the QMG were running trials on various materials, but in view of the urgency they opted for the readily available HBT, a tightly woven material which at least provided good protection against insect bites - a serious factor, given the high incidence of disease under tropical combat conditions. The Model 1942 suit was issued in August of that year. Visible over his shoulder is the top of a camouflaged M1943 jungle pack.

(Left) The M1942 jungle suit had a full length zipper at the front, concealed by a flap with a single snap fastener at the throat. The two large chest pockets were secured with flaps each with two snap fasteners, as were the cargo pockets mounted high on the outside of each thigh. Both chest and thigh pockets were of the bellows or expanding gusset type, enabling the GI to carry bulky items. Cloth suspenders, shown here, were sewn inside the suit to enable the crotch to be raised or lowered to prevent chafing, and to distribute the the weight of heavily loaded thigh pockets. In the field the suspenders were usually cut out, as they were uncomfortable on the shoulders, despite the fact that the suit had a bi-swing back to ease shoulder movement. The wrists were secured by a tab to a metal button.

(Right) Carrying an M1942 machete, this GI wears the M1942 jungle suit with the trousers rolled loose over M1938 leggings and service shoes. Although the suit was camouflage-printed in shades of green on one side and brown on the other, the design of the pockets and suspenders meant that it was not, in fact, reversible - unlike the US Marine Corps' two-piece jungle suits, which could be worn with either side outwards. As with the one-piece mechanic's overall, this garment was unpopular with the troops: since it had no back flap they had to shuck all their webbing gear and virtually undress to answer the insistent calls of nature which, under the conditions of the Pacific theater, were a fairly regular occurence.

(Left) A jungle raider wears the kind of light, improvised patrol dress not uncommon in the Pacific. He wears a short-visored M1941 HBT cap in faded OD, an officer's khaki cotton shirt without insignia, and Army issue cotton shorts; normally used for recreation in rear areas, these shorts had a patch pocket at the rear, a watch fob pocket, and an integral belt with a tongueless metal buckle. His minimal equipment includes an M1936 pistol belt, and an early canvas bag for the 50-round Thompson drum magazine, behind which is an M1924 first aid pouch; and he has slung on a captured Japanese canteen. He is armed with the M1928A1 Thompson sub-machine gun fitted with a drum magazine. The canvas M1908 Keer rifle sling, dating from WWI, was commonly fitted to the Thompson.

(Right) A late version of the tropical fibre helmet worn to some extent in rear areas. The early version of this moulded helmet was covered in pale OD material; this later example has a greener shade of covering. Note the narrow chinstrap tucked up over the front brim.

(Left) *Detail of the 18in. M1942 machete in its canvas scabbard; and the US Army's experimental two-quart collapsible water container.*

(Above) *Not every US soldier had a Colt .45 semi-automatic. Here, a GI loads a Smith & Wesson .38 cal. six-shot revolver. Note the leather M1897 revolver holster which does not clip to the eyelets of the pistol belt like most US belt loads, but has a broad suspension loop to slip over it. Note the belt's triple row of eyelets; it also features a male snap fastener to engage with the female fitment on the M1923 pistol magazine pocket.*

(Left) A GI in action during one of the 1944 Pacific island battles. He wears the standard Pacific theater combat dress for most of the war - the two-piece OD shade 7 herringbone twill work suit, in this case with the trousers worn loose over the 1942 canvas and rubber jungle boots.

He carries his gear in the M1943 jungle pack, with an M1910 E-tool and an M1942 18in. machete - here an example cut down to a more manageable length - attached to it. His M1936 pistol belt supports an M1910 canteen and a jungle first aid pouch, to which is hooked the pale tan M1942 first aid pouch. He is armed with the M1 .30 cal. carbine with a 15-round magazine and, just visible under his left armpit, a MkIIA1 fragmentation grenade.

The M1943 jungle pack was a great improvement over the M1928 haversack. Its capacity was significantly greater and more versatile, it provided better protection for the contents, and was more comfortable to wear. The small zippered pouch on the top was used to carry items that the soldier might need to get at quickly without unpacking the main bag; and the drawstring closure of the pack, under the flap, made it easy to pack. The narrow vertical and horizontal straps allowed the pack to be enlarged or contracted according to contents.

(Right) A close-up of the green jungle first aid pouch, to which is hooked a standard issue M1942 first aid pouch. The latter, hardly changed since WWI, carried a basic field dressing sealed in a brass can painted either red or, from mid-1943, OD. The jungle pouch was adopted in August 1943; it held dressings, plasters, tubes of burn ointment, a bottle of insect repellent, a tourniquet and a spatula.

(Right) A soldier wearing the two-piece HBT suit and the short-visored M1941 HBT fatigue cap, armed with the M1911A1 .45 cal. Colt semi-automatic.

(Left) The two-piece HBT was relatively light and practical, allowing better circulation of air and greater convenience than the ill-conceived one-piece jungle suit. In its simplified version produced during 1943 the jacket lacked the two-button added waistband and buttoned cuffs of the first pattern, and the pockets were squared off; and the trousers acquired a large cargo pocket high on the outside of each thigh. The first M1943 trousers had bellows expansion gussets at rear and bottom only of the cargo pockets; this man wears the second pattern, with a central expansion pleat.

(Left) Caught in the act of throwing a MkIIA1 fragmentation grenade, this soldier wears the two-piece HBT suit with the trousers worn loose - for better ventilation, and to avoid trapping water in the legs - over canvas leggings and service shoes. Combat gear was, typically, lightened to a minimum whenever possible in the Pacific, to save weight and heat; here it consists merely of an M1923 cartridge belt to which is clipped an M1942 canteen and, stuffed under the belt at the back, an M1910 T-handle entrenching tool.

(Above) Part of an infantry squad, all wearing the M1943 two-piece HBT suit. The GI nearest the camera has an M1943 jungle pack in Army camouflage material, with an M1943 entrenching tool and an M1942 machete. Next to him kneels a soldier with the M1943 jungle pack in plain OD, to which he has attached an M1910 pick-mattock in its canvas carrier. He is armed with the squad's .30 cal. M1918A2 Browning Automatic Rifle, and wears the M1937 ammunition belt with six pouches each holding two 20-round BAR magazines. Note his M1943 combat boots. The furthest man has the camouflaged jungle pack and, in place of the M1 helmet, wears the short-visored M1941 HBT cap.

Mediterranean Theater:

Operation "Torch"

On 8 November 1943 Operation "Torch" put US troops ashore in French North Africa. Brief fighting against some Vichy French garrisons was soon followed by the advance into Tunisia, and the US Army's first encounters with the German Wehrmacht.

The US Army had not anticipated the great variation in temperature found in North African coastal regions, and particularly in the Tunisian mountains. The troops landed with temperate climate gear – HBTs, OD field jackets, wool trousers – and soon learned that the nights could be freezing and the rain incessant. By mid-winter they had piled on every sweater, overcoat and raincoat they could find, and lived for many days at a time without climbing out of their long woollen drawers and undershirts. To their natural inclination toward casualness in field dress was added the example of the British desert troops alongside whom they fought, and whose individuality of dress was legendary. General George S. Patton, who took over II Corps after the Kasserine defeat, used strict dress regulations enforced by fines as one way of restoring discipline: officers and men alike were fined for even discarding the necktie in the front lines.

(**Above**) This GI wears the standard dress and equipment of the landing phase of this campaign. The jacket of the M1942 two-piece herringbone twill suit had two patch chest pockets with clipped corners and flaps, secured with single buttons. He wears the M1923 cartridge belt and M1928 haversack, and slung across his chest is the service gasmask; over his shoulder he carries the M1 .30 cal. semi-automatic rifle on an M1907 leather sling. Note the thick, fabric-covered fibre liner visible under his M1 helmet. On his left arm he displays a US flag brassard; this kind of quick identification, in various materials and patterns, was worn in a number of campaigns where US and Allied troops were operating together in a combat environment.

(**Left**) Both men wear the two-piece herringbone twill suits, with M1938 canvas leggings and service shoes. Both have the M1942 jacket, but the left hand man wears experimental M1943 trousers with patch cargo pockets on the thighs. His M1936 pistol belt supports an M1924 first aid pouch and, on the right hip, the five-pouch magazine pocket for his Thompson M1928A1 .45 cal. sub-machine gun. On his left hip is his gasmask.

(Far left) Another view of the typical GI uniform of the Moroccan and Algerian landings. Note the M1942 bayonet on the M1928 haversack.

(Left) Rear view of the Thompson-armed GI. Note the M1910 pick-mattock strapped to his M1928 haversack, the haft exposed and the curved head in a canvas carrier. Note the adjustment tab on the side of the M1942 jacket, and the flat cargo pockets on the thigh of the experimental M1943 HBT trousers.

(Below) Detail of the two different styles of HBT trousers. The 1942 pattern, left, has two hip pockets, the left one having a button closure, and no cargo pockets on the thigh. The experimental M1943 trousers, right, have no hip pockets, but a patch cargo pocket on each thigh. Note, left, the M1928 haversack and the M1910 entrenching tool.

(Above) The M1 Dust Respirator was issued to the crews of open vehicles and others for the "Torch" landings. It was a typically thoughtful "theoretical" piece of equipment, ignored and soon discarded by the troops as an over-complicated burden. Note also the pleated pockets of the early 1942 HBT jacket, its added waistband with two buttons, and detail of the blackened metal "13-star" buttons used throughout this suit, and most other US Army fatigue clothing items.

(Right) US Army service gasmask. The wearer breathed through the corrugated tube and a filter canister carried in the canvas satchel. Though carried by most armies throughout the war gasmasks were — in the absence of gas — an irritating and pointless burden, thrown out by any soldier who thought he could get away with it. Burial details were about the only troops who found a practical use for them.

Arctic & Mountain Dress

*I*n common with other armies, the US Army took seriously the possibility of having to commit its troops to cold, mountainous environments. A fairly comprehensive range of special clothing and equipment was designed and trialled, and it was anticipated that complete mountain divisions thus equipped and trained would soon be deployed to the appropriate fronts. In the event, the general shortage of combat infantry which increasingly plagued the Allies during 1944-45, and the practical impossibility of reserving any particular formation for action in a particular sector, led to a much vaguer picture. Units and formations such as the 1st Special Service Force and the 10th Mountain Division received certain items special to their anticipated role, but in combination with standard GI issue equipment. Pages 44-50 illustrate mountain and Arctic equipment mostly as it appeared during training in North America; although the simultaneous campaigns in different theaters make any strictly chronological chapter arrangement impossible, there is some logic to associate this equipment with the Italian campaign which follows.

(Right) Two GIs wearing the early kersey-lined tan cotton coat and trousers for Arctic operations, as they might have appeared in the Aleutians in 1942. The soldier on the left has the unlined M1941 poplin hood, which secured with a drawstring; it was issued for wear either under the M1 helmet or on its own. The man on the right wears the winter cap, an unpopular headgear originally issued for wear with the range of US Army mackinaws. The Arctic coat closed with a concealed zipper and five OD plastic buttons; note adjusment tabs at wrist and waist.

(Left) The mountain rucksack, developed from the Norwegian Bergen Norse Pac for mountain and ski troops and the 1st Special Service Force. Designed to hold several days' necessities for a GI in combat, it had three external strapped pockets and three webbing tabs with pairs of eyelets for hooking on tools, etc. The rucksack was mounted on a tubular steel frame with a waist strap to hold it steady on the march. It was stated that in an emergency two frames could be strapped to a pair of skis to make a sledge. This example is dated 1942.

(Right) A GI on a training exercise in the Rockies, wearing the mountain jacket of OD windproof cotton, an early model ski-mountain cap with chinstrap and fold-up ear/neck flaps, and mountain trousers; note also rucksack and mountain ice-axe. The jacket has two large expanding patch pockets on the chest, which are closed with a zipper under an unsecured flap. Two large interior-hung pockets in the jacket skirt are secured by single-button flaps. The front closure is a concealed zipper under a buttoned fly flap. The jacket has an attached hood and an integral pack in the back. It has a web belt at the waist, run through very broad loops, with a metal frame buckle. The cuffs are secured with tabs to paired buttons. All buttons are OD plastic.

(Left) Rear view of the mountain jacket, worn here with the hood up; the hood could be folded under the collar when not required. The waist belt is unfastened here, allowing the lower part of the integral pack to drop - it was stowed folded inwards and upwards under the belt. Note the opened zipper of the pack's side access. The trooper is taking the container for the M1942 one-burner stove from his rucksack.

(Below left) Preparing a meal, the GI sets up the M1942 one-burner stove from the mountain cookset; the two halves of the burner container can be seen at the top of the picture. It could also be packed in the main cookset can, right.

(Above) Detail of the inside of the mountain jacket. These integral suspenders helped adjust the ride of the load in the back pack.

(Right) *The trooper fastening a pair of mountain crampons to his ski-mountain boots. The boots are the second pattern, with heavily cleated rubber soles replacing the leather soles of the first pattern. Note his ski-mountain goggles with green-tinted glass lenses. The ski-mountain cap was later replaced by the M1943 cap.*

(Left) *The ski-mountain boots, worn with the 7in. canvas ski gaiters; these secured by a crossed leather strap passing under the instep and forward through the top center leather loop.*

(Above left) An instructor with a trainee ski-trooper. The instructor wears a five-button sweater over a pair of OD wool ski trousers (dated 23 June 1941); the broad single belt loop at the back is just visible. He has on a pair of shoepacs and a ski-mountain cap, and around his neck a pair of tinted goggles. The GI on the right has a reversible parka white side out, white overmittens, and white field overtrousers (dated June 1941). His rucksack has a white cotton cover fitted over it and secured with a drawstring. He wears webbing ski gaiters over his ski-mountain boots.

(Above right) The wool felt face mask, issued to troops to prevent frostbite, had a resinous treatment to prevent it absorbing moisture. It was reversible, to a dark blue on the inside, and had a deep flap which tucked down inside the neck of the clothing.

(Left) Detail of the deep three-button waistband which was one of the identifying features of the ski trousers. Obscured here by M1944 shoepacs, the lower legs and ankles tapered in and elasticated straps passed under the feet. The side pockets were fastened with zippers - the brass bead pull for the zip can just be seen below the GI's right hand. The two hip pockets had pointed buttoned flaps.

(Right) Detail of the white cotton helmet cover made for issue in snowy conditions - but in practice not always available in numbers when and where it was needed. During the 1944-45 Ardennes campaign in Belgium many of the GIs rushed into the line made snow camouflage ponchos and helmet covers out of sheets and table cloths for lack of anything better.

(Below left) The Arctic felt double-buckle boot was based on the Arctic felt snowshoe. These excellent boots were made with an inner sole of felt and a thin leather outer sole, but were not issued for combat.

(Below right) A pair of ice-creepers being fastened to the Arctic felt boots. These simple spiked plates, of which at least two different patterns existed, could be buckled round any type of footwear to improve grip in icey conditions.

(Left) The final pattern of mountain parka. This OD shade 7 cotton field parka, with fur-trimmed hood, had two angled slash pockets on the chest secured by pointed buttoned flaps; it was tightened by drawstrings at waist and hem. Unlike previous parkas, this type was not reversible; a white over-parka was available. We place it here in the book because sources differ over whether or not it was ever worn in combat before VE Day.

(Right) Detail of the pile liner issued with the last pattern parka; this was full-length, complete with sleeves and a trimmed hood.

Italian Theater

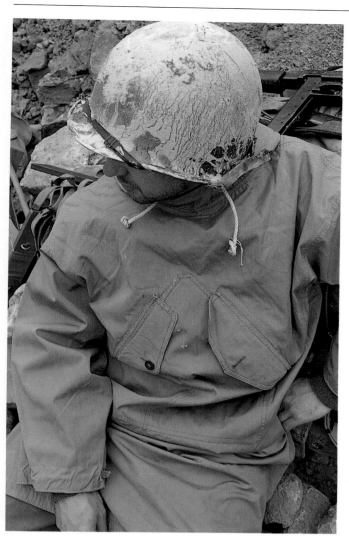

The 1st Special Service Force was activated on 20 July 1942, under Colonel Robert T. Frederick, and based at Fort Harrison, Montana. Formed from volunteers from the US and Canadian armies, the Force was intended for hit-and-run raids behind enemy lines, with an emphasis on winter mobility - their originally planned objectives were vital enemy installations in occupied Norway. Personnel were trained as paratroopers, amphibious commandos, mountain and ski troops, and the Forcemen became experts at demolition and sabotage.

The impractical Norwegian operation was subsequently scrapped; the 1st SSF participated in the US landings on Kiska in the Aleutians in August 1943, but this proved to be a bloodless victory. The Force was shipped to Italy in November 1943; and first went into action at Monte La Difensa in Kesselring's Winter Line on 3 December. The 1st SSF fought with distinction in Italy for nearly a year; and the photographs on pages 51-56 seek to recreate the appearance of Forcemen during this campaign, as exemplars of certain US Army mountain warfare equipment.

(Left) The deep-pointed, buttoned chest pocket flaps identify a variant of the first pattern parka with no fur trim to the hood or cuffs. The neck of the first pattern has no flap opening; the parka is pulled over the head like a smock and secured at the neck and wrists by drawstrings. Note the common practice of applying mud as camouflage to the M1 helmet.

(Below) Three types of parka. On the left, the ski parka (dated 14 July 1942) has a fur-trimmed hood, narrow buttoned flaps on the slash pockets, buttoned neck opening, buttoned wrist tabs and a drawstring at the hem. In the center is a first pattern parka with fur-trimmed hood and cuffs, no flaps to the pockets, and drawstring closures at neck and wrist. On the right is another view of the first pattern variant without fur trim, with deep buttoned pocket flaps, and drawstrings at neck and wrist. These parkas were all reversible to white. All the soldiers wear mountain trousers; the centre man has shoepacs and the other two paratrooper jump boots.

(Top right) Detail of the first pattern parka (dated 21 May 1941) with fur trim to hood and cuffs, no opening at the neck, drawstrings at neck and wrists, and diagonal chest pockets without flaps or fastenings.

(Below right) A GI wearing a ski parka over a pair of mountain trousers. His webbing includes the M1936 pistol belt with a twin-pouch M1923 pistol magazine pocket and a five-pouch magazine pocket for his M1 Thompson gun. Note the 30-round magazines in the 20-round pouches: a common expedient, since 30-round magazine bags were not available at this time. Note also that the magazine pouches are of composite man-ufacture, using the old tan webbing for the body but with flaps in distinctly greener material. Strapped to the side of his mountain rucksack is a V-42 Commando knife.

(Below) A Forceman sharpening his V-42 Commando (or "Stiletto") knife; this weapon was standard issue to the Force. Modelled after the British FS fighting knife, it was manufactured by Case; identifying features of this rare weapon are the "skull-crusher" pommel, leather washer grip with fine grooving, leather cushion above the slightly downcurved crossguard, and "thumbprint" on the ricasso. In the background is an A2 flight jacket; these were standard issue to the Force during their early training.

(Opposite page) This GI, demonstrating the bulk of the rucksack, wears the reversible ski parka, with fur trim at the hood but none at the cuffs, over OD wool shirt and trousers. He carries ammunition for his M1 rifle in a six-pocket cotton bandoleer and an M1923 cartridge belt, hung on which is his M1910 canteen. He has an M1910 T-handle en-trenching tool hooked to the tab on the left side of the rucksack.

(Left) A Forceman wearing a first pattern parka with fur trim and mountain trousers reloading the M1941 Johnson light machine gun which was one of the 1st SSF's peculiarities. Of particular interest is the scabbard for his V-42 knife. This extra long scabbard was designed so that the wearer could still reach the knife with comparative ease even if it were worn under the parka. It was made up for the Force by the makers of the US Marine Corps Stiletto, using surplus scabbards sewn to an M1910 belt hanger with a snap-fastened hilt strap sewn in; note the grommet at the bottom for a leg thong.

(Below) The left hand man wears a reversible parka-type overcoat with the hood up over his helmet. This parka, unlike all the previous types, opened the full length of the front, secured by five plastic buttons; three smaller plastic buttons secured the lower flap of the hood across the chin, and the hood could be pulled tight to the face by a drawstring. There were two large patch pockets with flaps on the front skirt of the coat, and two flapless slash pockets above these. The cuffs were secured by a deep, tapering tab buttoned back to paired buttons. Under the parka he wears M1943 HBT trousers tucked into M1938 leggings, over service shoes.

The Forceman at center is wearing the pile liner designed to be worn under the fully opening parka. Standing on his left is a GI wearing his parka (dated 24 July 1942) fully open. Under it he wears an M1943 field jacket buttoned to the neck beneath a pair of "tanker's" winter combat trousers. Note the white lining of the reversible parka/overcoat.

(Below left) 1st SSF Forceman wearing the pile liner designed to be worn under the fully opening parka/coat; in suitably snowy conditions where it would not show up the troops quite often wore this item on its own. Over it he wears an M1923 cartridge belt and M1936 suspenders in the later 1943 manufacturing shade (OD shade 7).

(Top right) The 1st Special Service Force patch. Although the Force comprised about 60% American and 40% Canadian personnel all wore US Army uniforms (with minor insignia distinctions for Canadian personnel on dress uniform). Note particularly the mountain trousers, worn with issue trouser suspenders; they have zipped pockets high on each side above large pleated cargo pockets on the thigh, and two flapped, buttoned rear pockets.

(Bottom right) The Yukon packboard was often seen in Italy, where much fighting took place in terrain inaccessible to anything larger than a mule. This back board, made from a wooden frame with a leather-reinforced canvas cradle, was used for carrying a variety of loads; this GI has an OD wool blanket under his mountain sleeping bag in its cover, and a cookset can on the top.

(**Above**) *1st SSF in action; the Force's six combat battalions were heavily armed with light weapons. Here the nearest man, wearing a Yukon packboard, is armed with the rare M1941 Johnson .30 cal. light machine gun. Each 1st SSF platoon had two sections; each section consisted of a sergeant section leader and a 2ic, both armed with Thompson guns; a Browning .30 cal. machine gunner and his assistant, and a 60mm mortarman and his assistant - in each team both men carried an M1 rifle, and the No.1 a .45 pistol; a Johnson gunner, and his rifleman assistant; a bazooka or flamethrower man, with rifleman assistant; and just two plain riflemen.*

(**Right**) *In the US Army the Johnson was unique to the 1st SSF, who had swapped two tons of RS demolition charges with the US Marine Corps in exchange for 125 of these guns. Unlike the BAR this weapon was able to fire either single shot or automatic. There is no evidence that the special magazine pockets for these guns ever reached the 1st SSF; spare 30-round magazines were carried wherever practical.*

Wherever the GI served he could be certain the medics would be close behind, to do all in their power to ensure the survival of the wounded. The emphasis placed on rapid recovery and treatment of casualties, and the availability of modern drugs such as penicillin and sulphonamides, reduced the rate of death among men wounded in battle to 4.5% - half the WWI rate.

(Below) *Italy, 1943-44: a casualty is prepared for evacuation. The PFC medic on the left, checking the casualty's "dog tags", has an OD field jacket, wool trousers, canvas leggings and service shoes. The medic on the right of the litter holding the plasma bottle wears the EM's M1938 raincoat with ventilated storm flap on the shoulders, wool trousers and M1943 combat boots. The GI in the left foreground, anxiously watching the treatment of his buddy, has on a winter combat jacket over a pair of winter combat trousers. On his M1928 haversack is an M1942 bayonet, and on his cartridge belt an M1910 canteen. The driver, fetching a dressing, wears an early issue M1943 field jacket over HBT trousers and leggings.*

(Right) *No room inside...A Dodge ³/₄ ton WC54 4x4 ambulance carries a medic on the running board, giving a clear view of one of the paired medical bags worn on a yoke harness. Note also the five-gallon water can on the ambulance wing; these are distinguishable by the large "flip-up" cap from the otherwise similar US gas cans, which had screw caps.*

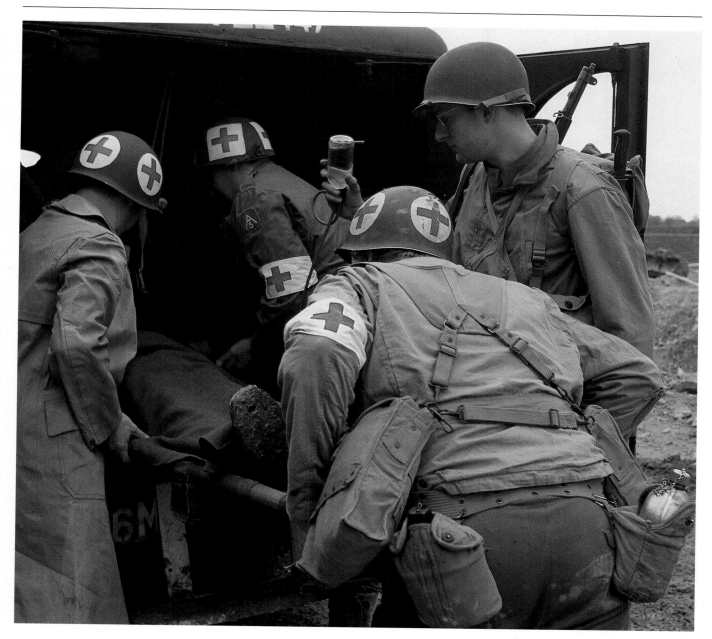

(Left) Fed up and far from home: a medic sits on the running board of a Dodge WC54 ambulance. He wears an OD field jacket with wool trousers, wool shirt and five-button sweater. His webbing consists of the special medic's harness yoke which supports a bag on each hip. On his helmet is painted the international recognition symbol for medical personnel, repeated on the brassard on his left arm.

(Above) The casualty is loaded into the ambulance by medics. Clearly seen here is the special medic's yoke with two bags; this medic also follows normal practice by carrying two canteens (here an M1942 and an M1910) on his pistol belt, giving him extra water for casualties. Note another angle on the M1938 EM's raincoat. Note the 5th Army patch on the driver's M1943 jacket; and the two different styles of medic's helmet marking.

(Right) Double-checking the details they have written on the GI's wound label with the information on his "dog tags".

(Below right) Identification "dog tags". The first line gave the name; the second his Army serial number (prefixed "O" for officers), inoculation record and blood type; the third, fourth and fifth the name and address of his next of kin, and at the right "C","P" or "H" for Catholic, Protestant or Hebrew. In 1944 the next of kin details were discontinued. The original M1940 tags were worn on a cord about 40ins. long. In 1943 the chain with 1.5in. extension was issued; this extension and one tag were removed at burial, the second tag remaining on the corpse. Note that the chain has flat links, not the later "bead" links.

(Left) An infantryman in Italy, 1944, wearing a winter combat jacket over winter combat trousers (dated 9 January 1942). His cartridge belt is in the greener shade of OD (No.7) used for webbing from 1943. Note the details of the six-pocket cotton ammunition bandoleer. Taken by surprise at the severity of the first winter in Italy, the US Army issued any available warm clothing. Although the winter combat jacket and trousers are commonly associated with tank crews, who wore them extensively, they were intended to be for general issue. The jacket was often worn by infantry; the trousers, which were cumbersome, less often.

(Below left) The M2A1 training gasmask, with the filter canister attached directly below the facepiece, was used as a stop-gap between the cumbersome early service issue and the later M4 light-weight type.

(Below right) To keep dirt from his M1 rifle this infantryman fits on the canvas muzzle cover, which is secured by a tab and two press studs. This was later replaced by a plastic disposable cover.

(Right) Late 1944: GIs of the 10th Mountain Division climb an Italian hillside under the burden of a water-cooled M1917A1 Browning .30 cal. machine gun, its tripod and 250-round ammo boxes, broken down into loads for the M1944 packboard, made of curved plywood with webbing inside to cushion the back. They display a typical mixture of combat clothing: mountain jackets and trousers, M1943 field jackets, liners and trousers, OD wool trousers, M1943 combat boots and shoepacs. The man furthest from the camera wears the mountain jacket, OD wool trousers, and heavy white socks turned down over shoepacs - a common sight in this division. The machine gunners wear holstered M1911A1 pistols and have acquired .30 cal. M1 carbines in place of rifles.

(Below left) 10th Mountain Division, Italy, 1944: infantryman wearing the mountain jacket over wool trousers.

(Below right) The pile field jacket was issued as the liner for the M1943 field jacket, and officially was not supposed to be worn alone except under shelter. It is worn here over mountain trousers (dated 11 September 1942). The jacket is made of OD shade 7 cotton poplin and fully lined with brown-grey alpaca pile; it has six cord loops fastening to large plastic buttons, two slash side pockets, and OD knit collar and cuffs similar to those of the winter combat jacket.

European Theater:

D–Day, 6 June 1944

At dawn on 6 June 1944 the largest armada in history landed its troops on the shores of Normandy; the Allied liberation of Europe had finally begun, after years of preparation and months of rehearsal. Some 200,000 American, British, Canadian and other Allied troops crossed the English Channel, while 24,000 airborne troops flew above them in transports and gliders. The last-minute gap in prevailing bad weather, which allowed General Dwight D.Eisenhower to risk ordering the postponed landings to go ahead, were made in choppy seas. Most of the troops were seasick as they churned towards the beaches in lurching, pitching landing craft; a comment was made at the time that the landings had been successful because "the troops would rather have faced thousands of the enemy before going back onto the boats and being sick again". (The US Army did try to give the GIs seasickness pills, but a veteran of the 29th Division recalled that after taking two as instructed, by midday he was staggering like a drunk and could hardly see. This is unsurprising: one of the ingredients was a powerful sleeping powder.)

On the American beaches the 4th Infantry Division landed on "Utah" and the 1st and 29th on "Omaha" ; and it was on "Bloody Omaha", in the face of savage enemy resistance, that the worst losses were suffered on 6 June - 2,000 of the total of 4,500 American casualties that day.

Our reconstructions **(previous pages, above, and right)** of the clothing worn during the landings show GIs of the 29th Division wearing the two-piece herringbone twill fatigue suit, canvas leggings and service shoes. They have M1928 haversacks, M5 assault gasmasks in black waterproof bags, and US Navy M1926 lifebelts over their webbing; their rifles are protected by plastic covers. The light-colored brassards worn on the left upper arm were of a chemically treated material which reacted visibly in the presence of poison gas - still a worrying threat to Allied planners at this stage of the war, although in the event neither side resorted to the use of gas as a battlefield weapon during World War II.

(Above) By D-Day armies had learnt to send troops ashore carrying the least possible burden, the heavy packs and duffle bags being brought ashore later. Nonetheless, the average GI carried a minimum of 70lbs of equipment through the surf, and his task was made no easier by the fact that material such as HBT doubled in weight when soaked in water.

(Left) Pausing for breath, this GI wears a British-made example of the M1928 haversack; note the style of the strap tabs. (There was considerable cross-manufacture of both clothing and personal equipment between the US and British armies in World War II.) He has an M1910 T-handle shovel, and an M1942 first aid pouch and M1910 canteen on his belt. Note that his rifle is still in its plastic waterproof cover. Around his waist is a partially inflated M1926 US Navy lifebelt. These were issued for amphibious assaults and some river crossings, but were regarded more as a liability than a help. Already top-heavy with pack, ammunition and weapons, the GI who lost his footing in water found that a lifebelt worn so low down had a tendency to tip him face-down in the water rather than giving any practical support.

(Opposite top) Although rarely worn by troops other than the Rangers, the US assault vest was issued to men of the 29th Infantry Division for the Normandy landings. They were not popular, despite their theoreticallly rational design; they were heavy, hot, and required the soldier to shuck his entire equipment rather than letting him lay it aside piece by piece if desired. The vests were mostly discarded within a very short time of landing. Note the litter of discarded lifebelts, rifle covers, etc., around this D-Day infantryman wearing the vest over HBT jacket and trousers. (This particular suit has a detail variation in the use of hollow-center metal buttons.)

(Opposite bottom left & right) Front and rear views of the US assault vest, basically similar to the British "battle jerkin" upon which it was modelled.

Rangers

*B*ritish Commando units were first raised in 1940 to carry out raids on the enemy-held coasts of Europe. In 1942 General Lucian K.Truscott Jr., US Army, was sent to England to arrange participation by picked US troops in British raids. As a result, US Army Chief of Staff General George C.Marshall ordered the raising of a US commmando unit. On 19 June 1942 the 1st Ranger Battalion was activated in Northern Ireland under command of Major William O.Darby, and selected volunteers were soon under training with the Commandos in Scotland. (They took the name "Ranger" from the famous unit of light troops led by Captain Robert Rogers in the French and Indian War of 1755-1763: officially "His Majesty's Independent Company of American Rangers", they were popularly known as "Rogers' Rangers".) The 1st Battalion's baptism of fire came in July 1942, when 50 men of the unit accompanied the British Nos.3 and 4 Commandos and troops of the Canadian 2nd Division on the very costly large-scale raid on the French port of Dieppe (six were killed, four captured and seven wounded). The whole unit fought in North Africa; and provided cadres in April 1943 for new 3rd and 4th Battalions. This Ranger Force fought with distinction in Sicily and Italy, until being almost wiped out at Cisterna in January 1944.

The 2nd and 5th Rangers were raised in the USA in 1943 for service in Europe. The 2nd Bn. sailed for Normandy on the eve of D-Day, their objective being the battery of German 155mm heavy guns on the Pointe du Hoc, a clifftop position which menaced both "Omaha" and "Utah" beaches. Led by Lt.Col. James E.Rudder, D, E and F Companies scaled the almost vertical 100ft. cliffs against fierce opposition. On gaining the top they found the gun emplacements empty; the guns had been moved inland, where a patrol later found and destroyed them. The 2nd Rangers held out against counterattacks for two days until relieved by the 5th Rangers, who had landed at "Omaha".

(Above) A Ranger of the 2nd Battalion - "Rudder's Rangers" reaches back for the next section of a light-weight scaling ladder. The first wave ashore wore the lightest possible gear; over his OD field jacket and first pattern M1943 HBT trousers he wears only a pistol belt with a canteen and bayonet, and a slung M1 Thompson .45 cal. sub-machine gun with a long 30-round magazine. This man wears the Airborne jump boots quite commonly seen in Ranger units.

(Left and right) Another Ranger hands up a ladder section, then starts climbing after the point man. Over his HBT jacket and trousers, worn with leggings and service shoes, he wears a British-made example of the US assault vest, with an M1910 shovel strapped to the back, a canteen and wirecutters hooked to the left and right sides, and - visible in the lower side pockets - hand grenades still in their cardboard tubes. His M5 assault gasmask is strapped to his left thigh.

The third Ranger, steadying the bottom of the ladder on the left, has a US assault vest with attached T-handle shovel and M1942 first aid pouch, and an M5 gasmask strapped to his chest. He wears the OD field jacket and HBT trousers with paratrooper's jump boots, and is armed with an M1 rifle. Round his waist is a deflated US Navy M1926 lifebelt. Note the orange diamond Ranger patch, with unit number, painted on the back of his helmet; these were common in the 2nd and 5th Rangers, as were the white horizontal and vertical NCOs' and officers' rear helmet stripes.

(Left) Detail of a British-made US assault vest; others made of the same dark brown canvas as the British battle jerkin are found in photographs. Whether these vests ever saw combat use by US troops is open to debate. Both British and US assault vests were cut large round the waist to accomodate the lifebelt. They had quick-release straps at the front to enable the vest to be dumped in a hurry if the belt had to be inflated.

(Right & above right) Examining the M5 assault gasmask - here with the cover still taped over the canister filter - and clipping on its black waterproof case. There was no special position for this, and it was attached wherever convenient. Note the Ranger shoulder patch, worn only by the 2nd and 5th Battalions.

France, 1944

(Below) GIs, wearing the minimum of equipment, carry their entrenching tools attached to their M1936 suspenders. Note the mix of patterns: an M1943 tool, left, and an M1910, center. The man in the center wears a second canteen cover on his right hip, holding extra grenades; at this stage in the war no pouches had been made specifically for grenades. Both the nearer men each have two cotton bandoleers of .30 cal. ammunition in addition to that carried in their cartridge belts.

(Right) GIs in action in the Normandy bocage, June 1944, wearing the US Army M1942 two-piece camouflage suit. The 30th Infantry Division and the 17th Engineer Battalion of the 2nd Armored Division were among the few US units which wore this suit for a short time in Europe; the superficial similarity of its camouflage pattern to that of the opposing German Waffen-SS troops led to some tragic cases of mistaken identity, and the suit was withdrawn. The GI on the right wears a rare pair of studded boots, made for the US Army by the British. Note that the trousers are worn over the canvas leggings, fastened with a tab and button at the ankle.

(Left) Front and rear views of the US Army M1942 herringbone twill cammouflage jacket. It has two patch chest pockets with square-cut flaps fastened by two concealed buttons, and a gas flap inside the neck.

(Right) Detail of the gas flap inside a pair of M1942 HBT camouflage trousers (dated 3 June 1943). Note the large cargo pocket on each thigh, with a square flap secured by two concealed buttons.

(Right) This BAR man wears an extremely rare jacket to his two-piece camouflage suit. The label inside the left hand pocket reads:

BLOUSE SUIT SNIPERS
U.S.A. ETO
SPEC. U/144U
1944

Under the date it bears the broad arrow stamp indicating manufacture by a British contractor to the War Department. Note pocket details, hem drawstring, etc.

(Left) A GI carrying his M1942 HBT camouflage jacket (dated 3 June 1943) over his shoulder shows the brown inside pattern of the two-piece uniform. As with the Army one-piece camouflage suit, the two-piece was not, in fact, reversible, having pockets only on the "green" side.

(Above) The Normandy bocage consisted of narrow sunken lanes running between small fields divided by massive banked hedges and thick copses of woodland. It was nerve-wracking terrain: every hedge and ditch could hide an enemy sniper or machine gun.

At full strength - an unusual situation - the US infantry rifle squad comprised 12 men: one or two NCOs with Thompson guns, one .30 cal. Browning Automatic Rifle, one M1903 Springfield bolt-action rifle fitted for sniping or launching anti-tank grenades, and eight M1 semi-automatic rifles. These GIs wear the uniforms typically seen in summer 1944: M1 helmets with or without netting, OD field jackets, OD wool trousers or HBT trousers, leggings and service shoes.

(Left) Detail of the special EM's wool shirt, showing the gas flap at the throat. "Special" in a garment's designation meant that it had flaps to prevent blistering agents contacting the skin; the shirt also had these at the wrist opening. His rank is technician/5th grade; the class "technician" was established in January 1942 to allow specialist personnel to receive better rates of pay without a rise in rank.

(**Right**) *Quenching his thirst from his canteen, this GI wears the second version OD field jacket that appeared in May 1941. The specification was PQD No.20A, although it is commonly referred to as the "M1941 jacket". On this version a gusset was inserted under the armpit to improve arm movement, a third button was fitted to the skirt to add to the adjustment range of the tightening tabs, epaulettes were added, and the flaps were removed from the pockets.*

The OD field jacket proved less than ideal in the field. Originally intended to be worn under the Army greatcoat or raincoat, in practice it was usually worn without either, and did not provide sufficient warmth or rain protection. Its light colour led to a very grubby appearance in a short time, and also made its wearer very conspicuous. Both collars and cuffs frayed rapidly, and the zippers were easily broken. Despite these drawbacks, and despite the fact that the OD field jacket was officially withdrawn in September 1943, the lack of its replacement, the M1943 field jacket, meant that this ubiquitous garment was to soldier on, one of the symbols of "GI Joe", until the end of the war in Europe in 1945.

Note also the details of the wool knit cap.

(Right & below) An infantry squad leader or second-in-command, wearing the two-piece herringbone twill suit; these fatigues were often used as combat uniform in the ETO in warm weather. Note also the unusually large mesh of his helmet net. Just visible under his right arm, on his pistol belt, is a pair of M1938 wire cutters. His weapons include two MkIIA1 fragmentation grenades at his belt, a WP smoke grenade clipped in his chest pocket, and an M1928A1 Thompson sub-machine gun. This fired at a rate of 700-800 rounds per minute, and although no sub-machine gun is accurate at more than close range its heavy .45 cal. rounds and high rate of fire made it a useful weapon in the close encounter battles which could flare up in the thick summer cover of the bocage. Note the Cutts compensator on the muzzle of the Thompson; the slots cut into its top surface allowing the expelled gases to escape upwards, counteracting the gun's tendency to rise when fired on full automatic.

Seen from the back, the GI carries an M1943 folding entrenching tool in its carrier, and just under this can be seen the tip of the M6 leather scabbard for a trench knife. Slung at his left hip is the bag for carrying the 30-round Thompson stick magazines. Tucked over the back of his pistol belt - a favorite place to stuff temporarily unwanted clothing - is his OD field jacket; and on the right hip is his M1910 canteen.

(Top right) In action in the bocage, these infantrymen are armed with the M1 semi-automatic rifle (not generally referred to during World War II by the name of its maker, Garand). The man nearest camera has an early, thick fibre helmet liner just visible, and a light-weight gasmask case on his right hip.

(Bottom right) Loading an eight-round clip of .30 cal. ammunition into the M1 rifle. The metal en bloc clip was loaded into the magazine together with the cartridges, and was ejected when the action returned after the last round was fired. A lip on the magazine platform then prevented the action closing, giving visible warning that the weapon was empty. The loading process was simple and quick, but took practice before the soldier learned to avoid the characteristic injury known as "M1 thumb". The M1 was the first self-loading rifle to be adopted as standard by any of the world's armies. Note the MkIIA1 fragmentation grenade clipped to the rifleman's webbing.

(Left) Firing an M1918A2 .30 cal. Browning Automatic Rifle, this GI wears the OD field jacket over a two-piece suit of HBT. His web equipment consists of the M1937 automatic rifleman's belt with six pockets, each holding two 20-round BAR box magazines. His EM's raincoat is folded over the back of the belt. Clipped to the M1936 suspenders he has an M1936 field (musette) bag - a popular alternative to the M1928 haversack; at his right hip an M1910 canteen carrier accomodates the later M1942 canteen. The hinge of the BAR's buttstrap is visible at his shoulder. The BAR, weighing about 20lbs., fired 600 rounds per minute on fast auto or 350 on slow; it could not be selected to fire single shots. One man per infantry squad carried a BAR, with a rifleman assistant carrying two more belts of ammunition.

(Right) Blowing dust from the magazine lips before reloading his BAR, this GI clearly shows the magazine port and the broad wooden foregrip; note the M1907 leather sling. Demonstrated by its inventor, John Browning, in 1917, the BAR first saw action on 13 September 1918 with the AEF; in fact his son, Lt. Valentine Browning, used his invention during World War I. The modified M1918A2 of 1940 had a lighter bipod, and a buttstrap: a flat strip of metal hinged to the heel of the butt which, when turned back, rested on top of the firer's shoulder, so that when firing with the barrel supported he had both hands free to reload, etc. Although it came equipped with a folding bipod this only weighed down the barrel and was usually discarded. The BAR remained in service until after the Korean War.

(Far left) Fixing a MkIIA1 fragmentation grenade to the grenade launcher attachment on an M1 rifle. These launchers had an effective range of some 250 yards; although obviously dependant on the firer's eye and experience for such accuracy as they possessed, they did give the rifle squad a useful additional capability in the absence of the company's weapons platoon .

(Left) Bracing his foot in his rifle sling to get a steady aim, a GI of the 29th Infantry Division prepares to fire the grenade. Note that his chinstrap is not clipped round the back of his helmet, as was so often seen. The commanding general of the 29th, Major-General Gerhart, an ex-cavalry officer from World War I, was strongly opposed to this practice: he felt that it was too easy for a GI to lose his helmet when moving at the double or diving for cover, and insisted that his men wore the chinstrap on or near the point of the chin.

(Right) Although the war had only about a year to run, in 1944 many GIs were still going into action with their gear in the pre-war M1928 haversack, which suffered from several drawbacks. The long, narrow shape did not ride well on the back; the contents had to be pre-folded before packing, which made it difficult to stow in the dark; and there was no room inside the pack for either a coat or spare boots, which had to be strapped on the outside, exposing them to the wet. Note this GI has his EM's raincoat tucked over his cartridge belt on his left hip.

(Above) Home from home: a GI spring-cleans his M1 rifle while his buddy snoozes - the shallowness of this rifle pit is dictated by the water table. On the front lip of the rudimentary foxhole lies another M1 with spare clips. To the left of it can be seen the cardboard tubes in which hand grenades came packed; left of them, a light-weight gasmask bag, and a 1942 model canteen with black plastic cap; and left of that, an M1928 haversack with a bayonet attached. On the GI's raincoat to left rear is an M1910 aluminium canteen and his three K-ration boxes, one each for breakfast, dinner and supper. In the foreground another light-weight gasmask bag is used to lay out the rifle parts and cleaning kit.

(Right) Unfolding the M1943 entrenching tool. This folding shovel, copied from a German design, was more versatile than the M1910 T-handle tool, and more compact to carry.

(Right) A close-up of the combination tool from the M1 cleaning kit, together with the plastic bottle containing the oiler brush. The rod of the combination tool, when wrapped in cloth, was to clean the chamber; later versions had a stiff brush in place of this. The rolled cord is a pull-through; one end has a metal rod weight, and a piece of rag soaked in bore-cleaning fluid from the can on the left is attached to the other; the weight is dropped through the barrel and the cleaning rag pulled through after it. The can of bore cleaner was intended to fit in one of the pockets of an M1923 cartridge belt.

(Left) Detail of the eight-round en bloc *clips* of .30 caliber ammunition for the Garand M1 semi-automatic rifle. These loaded into the magazine complete with rounds, unlike those of Allied and enemy bolt-action rifles, whose charger clips were engaged with a guide above the open magazine before the rounds were pushed down into the magazine with a thumb and the clip was discarded.

(Right) Close-up of MkIIA1 fragmentation grenades with their cardboard storage tubes.

Fall/ Winter 1944

(Right) An infantry patrol leader moving cautiously forward wears his OD field jacket reversed - a practice confirmed by photographs and veterans - as the blanket lining gave a darker and less conspicuous appearance. He wears HBT trousers and has the short-billed M1941 HBT cap. He is armed with an M1 .30 cal. carbine, and the M3 trench knife in an OD plastic scabbard hangs at his hip. Under his left elbow can be seen a white phosphorous smoke grenade.

(Left) Patrolling infantrymen carried the minimum of kit: on the left, HBT trousers, wool shirt, a knit jeep cap and an OD field jacket worn inside-out. His companion wears the OD field jacket right side out; note its pale appearance in slanting evening sunlight. He has a wool shirt and scarf, wool trousers, wool and leather gloves, and the knit cap worn back to front. His weapon is the M3A1 .45 caliber sub-machine gun, nicknamed the "grease gun" from its appearance. Designed as a cheaper mass-production replacement for the heavy and expensive Thompson, and introduced to service during 1942, the M3 series fired 350-450 rounds per minute and took a 30-round box magazine. In readiness for firing he has opened the hinged cover which kept dirt out of the large ejector port while the gun was not in use.

(Left) Wearing the EM's wool overcoat, with brass buttons, this GI carries his M1 rifle slung over his shoulder together with an OD duffle bag. On his belt is hooked a pair of M1938 wire-cutters. The full length, double-breasted overcoat of OD wool melton was envisaged as a cold weather combat garment, and was so worn right through the last winter of the war in Europe due to the lack of sufficient supplies of true combat clothing in winter weights, but proved too cumbersome. High quality woollen material gives considerable warmth - except under extreme conditions there were surprisingly few complaints on this score even against the wool field uniforms worn in the World War I trenches; but when soaked, and particularly when the skirts get caked with mud, the greatcoat becomes oppressively heavy. This US Army model had a roll collar, epaulettes, and two internally hung slash pockets. The pleated rear had a fixed half-belt, secured by two buttons which allowed waist adjustment. There were three visible pairs on the front, and a fourth pair concealed under the deep lapels for fastening the collar and lapels across. All buttons were of brass, embossed with the US coat of arms.

(Below) Rear view of the EM's wool melton overcoat; left, of the M1937 BAR belt and M1936 suspenders; and, center, of the SCR-300/BC1000 man-pack radio carried by infantry platoon headquarters. Despite modern usage it was this radio set which was known as the "walkie-talkie" - the hand-held SCR-536/BC611 was the "handie-talkie".

(Left) A new kid on the block: a shiny young replacement, wearing the first examples of the M1943 field uniform and equipment that he has seen, is closely examined by an "old sweat" in a Belgian forest in the winter of 1944-45. Over the M1943 jacket and trousers he wears greenish web equipment in the 1943 "olive drab shade No.7". He carries the M1 rifle and on his feet he wears a pair of shoepacs. In addition to the 80 rounds carried in the ten pouches of the M1923 cartridge belt (or 96 in the briefly-manufactured 12-pouch M1938) he carries extra rifle ammunition in the two six-pocket cotton bandoleers across his chest. He has his wool overcoat rolled and stowed around the top of his M1944 combat field pack (see also pages 96-98). Note that the old hand wears a woollen hood under his helmet; originally designed as a protection against gas, it was in practice used in cold or wet weather.

(Below & opposite top left) The M1943 field jacket was the result of a wish by the US Army both to standardise a combat uniform in place of the variety of specialised combat clothing being worn by infantry, armored troops, paratroopers, mountain troops etc.; and to replace the less than satisfactory OD field jacket. It was decided to produce a uniform that would employ the "layering" principle, to suit both temperate and cold climates, depending upon the clothing worn beneath it. The Philadelphia Quartermaster Department first issued the jacket in May 1943, with the specification number PQD 370. It had a sateen shell with cotton lining, a detachable hood and, most importantly, four pockets; those on the chest were of the patch type and those in the skirt internal, and reinforced to enable the carrying of such items as grenades. Under the left collar was a tab to close the neck when the collar was turned up, and, unlike the OD field jacket, epaulettes were fitted from the outset. The fly front closed with six concealed buttons, and the wrist closure was also a button fastening. The waist was adjusted by an internal drawstring.

Succeeding modifications were minor. On PQD 370A the collar tab was moved up from the bottom edge of the collar to top, while PQD 370B saw the tab moved off the collar altogether, appearing instead as a large triangular tab stitched to the top of the jacket front. Under PQD 370C another button was

added to the jacket top to hold down the collar tab when not in use.

The M1943 trousers were intended as over-trousers, to be worn over pile-lined trousers or the OD wool uniform trousers; in the event they were mostly worn over the latter. Made from sateen cloth, the first version, PQD 371, appeared in June 1943. Fitted with two slash pockets both front and rear, they were equipped with both belt loops and buttons for braces (suspenders) and also had a waist-tightening tab on either side. There was a cargo pocket fitted to the right leg. This was to be discarded very soon with the introduction of the PQD 371A, and a small "ruler" pocket was substituted. Specification PQD 371B saw this pocket removed as well, in February 1944. Variants of the trousers include garments fitted with metal buttons rather than fibre, and some trousers made from herringbone twill. Some pairs of M1943 trousers have been found with a "field mod" carried out by US paratroopers; these will be

found to have a large cargo pocket stitched to each thigh.

The M1943 cotton field cap appeared at about the same time as the uniform; in OD 7 material, with a fold-down internal ear and neck flap with a soft lining, it was intended to replace the M1941 knit cap for use under the helmet.

The issue of the M1943 uniform never kept up with expectation. Production was already lagging behind when, in 1944, it was deliberately held back in favour of the new wool ETO or "Ike" jacket; in the European theater it was expected that the Ike jacket would be readily available, but this, in turn, also fell behind, and even where available was almost never worn as a field garment. The M1943, though originally intended for issue only to the paratroopers in Europe, slowly became the standard combat jacket, though these problems over its supply meant that the old OD field jacket would continue to be worn by many troops until VE-Day.

(Above) In use, the M1943 jacket was much superior to its predecessor, and the size and positioning of the four pockets prompted one commanding officer to joke that his men could "live out of their pockets for a week". There was some inconsistency in the issue of the jacket, the hood, and the pile liner (or pile field jacket as it was officially termed - see page 61) ; troops who had not received the liner complained that it was not warm enough, and others complained of the lack of waterproofing when wearing it in the rain. Some, though issued with the M1943, still wore their old "tankers'" winter combat jackets, claiming that they were much warmer. These were fairly minor and infrequent complaints on the whole; and it is a testament to the jacket, and the principle of "layering" combat clothing, that virtually all major armies now use combat jackets whose design can be traced back to the M1943.

(Right) An infantry lieutenant platoon commander with his radioman. Note officer's white vertical bar field recognition sign on the back of his helmet. He wears an M1943 field jacket (dated 1 August 1944), wool trousers, and felt overboots over M1943 combat boots. On his back is an M1936 field bag, attached to M1936 suspenders. This is a late version - unusually, still made from the early, pale OD shade 9 material - with an eyeletted tab attached to the flap for carrying entrenching tools, etc. The M1936 field or "musette" bag had two short straps at the top rear with snap fasteners to fix it to either a sling or the M1936 suspenders. Used to carry meat cans, rations, ponchos, toilet articles, spare socks and other items of clothing, and issued to officers, mountain troops and motorised units, it was a popular and widely "liberated" item throughout the Army. On his belt, from right to left, are a holstered .45, M3 trench knife, canteen, M1942 first aid pouch and M1917 binocular case. On the left is his M1938 dispatch (map) case.

(Above right) His radioman wears the EM's wool overcoat, wool trousers and shoepacs. He too is armed with the M1 carbine. Note that the lieutenant's rank bar on the front of the officer's helmet is much smaller than the stripe on the back - the latter bore no relation to specific rank.

(Left) The officer wears OD wool gloves with russet leather palms, as he consults his marching compass. The compass pouch is open, left of the belt buckle; right of it is the two-pouch pocket for 15-round carbine magazines.

(Right) After marching, the next best thing that a "dogface" gets to do is digging. These GIs are digging "scrapes" with M1943 entrenching tools; with the swivel blade held in this alternative position by the neck locking ring it could be used in the "pick" mode.

(Above) Two GIs take cover behind a shell-splintered tree. The left hand man wears the M1943 jacket with a woollen scarf and British-made wool knit gloves. The BAR gunner has the dark shade OD wool trousers.

(Left) Huddled in his "scrape", this rifleman wears the M1943 field jacket with the hood attached. This was designed large, to be worn over the Ml helmet if desired; it buttoned to the jacket under the collar and epaulettes, and had a drawstring and buttoned flap to close it tightly around the face. He has wool trousers and M1943 combat boots, and wears an M1928 haversack.

(Above) The GI sitting with his back to the camera has the M1943 EM's double texture raincoat (dated November 1943) with the ventilated reinforcement on the shoulders. Standing at left is a man with the early resin-coated type (dated 9 June 1942); standing at right is a GI with the synthetic rubber-coated version. The lieutenant has the officer's quality double texture OD raincoat (dated 9 December 1944); this has epaulettes, an integral belt, and all-round buckled strap cuff adjusters. The raglan sleeve of the seated GI's coat was more effective at keeping out water than the coat-style seam on the other two coats.

(Right) Another view of the M1943 synthetic rubber-coated EM's raincoat. Note the rounded shape to the internally hung pockets as compared with the square patch pockets of the earlier M1938 pattern coat.

(Left) A GI wearing a first pattern mackinaw, of a greenish cotton duck instead of the more usual tan color; an M1941 wool toque; and 18oz wool serge trousers OD 33, special (dated June 1943) – note the adjusting tabs on the inside of the leg. A pair of trigger-finger mittens lie next to his newly issued M1943 combat boots; these have reversed uppers and one-piece composition soles.

(Above) Three different styles of US Army issue sweater. The GI with the magazine (apparently expressing some reservations about the practical application of the article on housekeeping in a foxhole) wears the best-known version, with long sleeves, a low stand-up collar and five plastic buttons; this example is a variation on the standard in that the collar buttons back to a pair of buttons sewn level with the top button hole. Center is an example of the sleeveless crew-neck sweater; and the GI on the left has the pattern with long sleeves and a V-neck.

(Above) The first and second pattern mackinaws. On the right is the first pattern with OD wool facing to the collar (dated 1938), made from cotton duck. On the left is the second pattern without the wool facing (dated August 1942), made from cotton poplin.

(Right) The third and final version of the mackinaw. The belt and belt loops have been deleted and the collar has notched lapels. This coat, (dated 1943) is made of cotton poplin.

Into Germany

*I*n March 1945 the Allies crossed the Rhine and began slashing into the industrial heart of the Third Reich. Although the ever-increasing material superiority and mobility of the US Army over the Wehrmacht left no doubt as to the eventual outcome, the German soldier was usually brave, stubborn and skilful in the defense of his own soil. Each day brought new advances; but each check along the way to deal with some scraped-together German battlegroup cost more lives. The Western allies were seriously short of infantry; mauled formations were broken up to reinforce others rather than being brought back to strength, and US infantry units were receiving some replacements with as little as three months' basic training. These green soldiers were often sent straight into battle without any time to become familiar with either their environment or their comrades, and suffered accordingly. The ordeal of combat for the infantryman, veteran or raw replacement, never eased until the very last shots were fired.

(Top left) Except for the second from left, these GIs hitching a ride on an M4 Sherman all wear the M1943 jacket over M1937 light OD wool trousers; the exception still wears an OD field jacket. Note the gusset in the open cuff of the M1943 on the left. The wooden box with rope handles, left, contains 24 grenades; and that next to it, 265 rounds of .50 cal. ammunition.

(Left) This military policeman directing troops along one of the axes of advance wears the OD field jacket of the first modified version issued in 1941, with no flaps on the slash pockets and added epaulettes. Slung across his chest is the M1938 dispatch case. His helmet is marked with a broad white band broken by the letters "MP" at the front, and he wears the white-on-dark-blue MP brassard on his left arm. Note the OD plastic whistle on a chain to his left lapel. His motorcycle is a Harley-Davidson WLA; mounted to the front fork is a leather scabbard for his M1 Thompson sub-machine gun; strapped to the scabbard is an M1910 T-handle entrenching tool.

(Above) The outskirts of yet another village, half-wrecked by preparatory artillery fire, and yet another scatter of shots from cover. The infantry disembark in a hurry to skirmish forward; in close country the tanks rely entirely upon the foot-sloggers to probe resistance - almost blind, they are all too vulnerable to concealed anti-tank guns and lurking Panzerfaust tank-killer teams. Field-crafty infantry will put distance between themselves and the Sherman as quickly as possible: its comforting bulk of steel is an illusion, and it is likely to draw the worst fire. Typically, the lack of space in the M1928 haversack obliges the GIs to carry their raincoats folded over their belts.

(Above & left) No matter how plentiful the artillery available to support the infantry and tanks, and no matter how completely the Allied air forces rule the skies: every last rubble-pile, if it is defended, must ultimately be taken by a guy with a rifle.....

Allied propaganda made much of the fact that untrained teenagers and unfit middle-aged fathers were being called to the defense of Germany. But, as one GI pointed out, he didn't care if his enemy was a hundred years old and riddled with disease - dug in behind formidable defences, he still had enough fingers left to pull a trigger.

(Right) The job has been done, hopefully without casualties among their close buddies; battle-hardened and resigned, the GIs saddle up and pull out - for the next bitterly held rubble-pile. They show one defiant touch of optimism: note the baseball bat and catcher's mitt on the left rear deck of the tank.

(Right) Preparing for a river crossing in Germany, spring 1945, this GI of a company's heavy weapons platoon, or a battalion's heavy weapons company, carries an M9A1 bazooka. He has an M1943 pack (despite being popularly known as the "jungle" pack, it saw service in the ETO redesignated simply as the M1943 field pack) with an M1 bayonet strapped to it. Close examination of his M1923 cartridge belt shows that two different shades of OD canvas have been used: the belt and flaps are made from M1910-type pale OD shade 9 but the pockets from green M1943-type shade 7. Manufacturers often used up existing stocks of older material before switching, and mixed-construction items are not very uncommon.

(Below) The GI on the left wears the new M1944 combat and cargo pack, with a blanket roll over the top. This pack was standardised in July 1944, after prolonged arguments between Army Ground Forces and the Office of the Quartermaster General over the best way to replace the M1928, for which previous contracts were finally completed in spring 1943. The new design was heavily influenced by the US Marine Corps M1941 pack; its major feature was two-part construction, with essential items carried in the upper or combat pack, and a detachable cargo pack with e.g. spare clothing and other non-essentials, which could be unbuckled and left with the rear echelon.

The man in the center has an M6 bag, which holds three of the bazooka's rocket projectiles in their cardboard packing tubes.

(**Above**) *Inflating the Navy M1926 lifebelt; these GIs are, in fact, using the emergency procedure for blowing up the belt. Note the two metal caps at the front of the belt on the right; these are for the insertion of small CO2 cylinders, which inflate the belt when screwed fully home - presumably the lines of supply have contrived to lose them in this case.*

The whole squad wear M1943 field jackets over OD wool or HBT trousers. The soldier at left has a three-pocket grenade pouch hooked to his belt on his right hip; this late-war item was the first purpose-made pouch issued for grenades. Watching the proceedings with some amusement, but not apparently with enough faith in the lifebelt to think his worth inflating, another bazooka man holds his launcher broken down in halves for transport. He has a multi-purpose extra ammunition bag slung on his left hip.

(**Right**) *Detail of an M9A1 late pattern 2.36in. rocket launcher or bazooka, dismantled for carrying by disengaging a locking collar at the midpoint. With skill, nerve, and luck the bazooka gave the infantry weapons platoon the ability to penetrate up to 4¹/₂ins. of armor plate at up to 700 yards' range - though much closer range was needed for a certain tank-kill.*

(Left) The M1944 cargo pack being unclipped from the combat pack, using the three quick-release straps. The former was a single compartment bag, with a top carrying handle; the latter had internal divisions, eyeletted tabs on the flap and left side, a small external pocket on the right side, and three straps for attaching a bedroll; both parts had rubberised fabric collars. This improved pack system was not issued in great numbers before the end of the war; a development of it was standardised as the M1945 pack.

(Top) The new light-weight gasmask was less bulky than its predecessor; it was a novelty, however, to find a gasmask bag containing one - GIs mostly used them as useful extra stowage space for the important little things of life - cigarettes, soap, dry socks, etc. The man on the left has the late-war close mesh helmet net and attached neoprene elastic band.

(Above) The light-weight gasmask in place.

Support Weapons

A complete breakdown of the distribution of weapons amongst an Infantry Division would require much more space than this book allows, but some of the weapons in this section would theoretically be found in the following numbers in the sub-units of a standard infantry regiment:

Three squads each with 11 rifles and sub-machine guns and one BAR, and a headquarters, made up the rifle platoon. Three rifle platoons and a weapons platoon, plus a headquarters (which included three medics from the battalion medical section) made up the 193-man rifle company. The weapons platoon had two .30 cal. light machine guns, one .50 cal. heavy machine gun, three 60mm mortars and three bazookas. Three such companies, plus a heavy weapons company and an HQ company, made up an 871-man battalion. The weapons company had eight .30 cal. machine guns, three .50 cals., six 81mm mortars, and seven bazookas; the HQ company, a three-gun anti-tank platoon with 37mm (later, 57mm) weapons. Three battalions and various regimental units made up a regiment, the latter including an anti-tank company with 12 guns

and a mine-laying platoon, and a cannon company with six short 105mm towed howitzers.

(Right) A paratrooper with the M1 bazooka in North Africa, 1943. Note the face mask used to protect him from the back-flash of the rocket launcher; this was a face-veil added to the M1943 disposable goggles. Just visible in the wooden butt is an indentation which housed a small lightbulb; in the case of a misfire, the GI checked to see if the bulb was lit - if it was, this meant the firing circuit was operative and he had a dud rocket.

(Below) The first 1941 pattern M1 2.36in. rocket launcher or bazooka, with the M6 rocket carrying bag.

(Above) A bazooka team, with an M9A1 rocket launcher, stalk a tank. The Number 2 is taking one of the 3.4lb. rockets from its cardboard container, while his Number 1 sights the weapon.

(Left) Loading a rocket into the tube. The Number 2 holds down the catch with his right hand to allow him to insert the round; this catch prevented the rocket slipping out backwards once loaded. Note that the Number 1 is wearing an M1943 pack.

(Right) The bazooka is ready to fire. A close look will reveal the thin ignition wire which the Number 2 has unwound from the rocket tail and attached to the electric contact on the right side of the firing mechanism. The loader must now move smartly away from the rear of the bazooka, to avoid the back-blast of the rocket, before tapping his Number 1's helmet in the "ready" signal. Note the three-pocket grenade carrier; each pouch held two grenades.

(Inset) Adjusting the sights on a bazooka; the protective cap on the eyepiece has been opened, and the graticule in the glass is just visible. Note the locking collar just ahead of the sights, where the bazooka could be separated into two halves for carrying.

(Left & below) A Browning .30 cal. gun team move out; at a total weight of 31lbs. the Browning broke down into two practical man-loads. They both wear two-piece HBT suits, and have added strips of burlap "scrim" to their helmet netting. Both have M1936 pistol belts and suspenders, and M1 carbines as individual weapons; the soldier carrying the Browning barrel has twin-magazine pockets on his belt and fixed round the butt of the weapon; the GI carrying the tripod also has a holstered M1911A1, and its M1923 twin-magazine pocket.

(Below) The Browning M1919A4 air-cooled .30 cal. light machine gun of the infantry weapons platoons and companies, fed by 250-round canvas belts carried in metal cans. With a rate of fire of 450-500 rounds per minute, this reliable weapon was effective against most infantry positions and all unarmored transport, though it could not punch through brick walls and light armor plate like the .50 cal. Browning.

(**Below & bottom**) *The Browning M2 HB .50 cal. heavy machine gun, issued to infantry weapons platoons and companies, originally with the primary role of anti-aircraft defense but in practice a devastatingly effective ground support weapon with a range of up to 1½ miles. HB stands for "heavy barrel", a modification which cured the tendency of the original model to overheat after about 80 rounds had been fired. Note the large ammo cans, and empty shells and links on the ground. The "Big 50" fired 450-575 rounds per minute and was fed with metal disintegrating-link belts of 105 rounds. It was deadly to almost all infantry positions, and "soft-skinned" transport, and could penetrate light armored vehicles such as half-tracks. At 84lbs. weight it could only be man-carried short distances.*

(Left) At 42lbs. the M2 60mm mortar was a heavy but possible load for one man for short marches, as this GI proves - note that the weapon is slung completely assembled except for the sight, with bipod folded against the tube and baseplate in place. Until the last moment all support weapons were carried on unit vehicles. Note the poncho-style ammunition bags worn by the soldier in the background.

(Below) Taking a 60mm mortar bomb from the M2 ammunition bags. Note the GI's slung M1 carbine, with two-magazine pocket fixed round the butt on a web sleeve; and the M1918 trench knife with knuckle-duster guard, worn here in an M6 leather scabbard rather than its purpose-made pressed metal sheath. These knives, often carried by paratroopers, were sometimes issued to members of weapons platoons.

(Page 105 top left) Sighting the 60mm mortar with the M4 sight.
(Page 105 top right) A lieutenant of a 29th Infantry Division weapons platoon takes personal charge of one of his mortar sections, using the SCR-536 "handie-talkie" to co-ordinate fire. The square leather case just visible behind the M17 binocular case is for the M4 mortar sight. Note the M1918 pistol magazine pocket on his belt; and the single rank bar pinned to his right shirt collar.

(Page 105 bottom) Laying down fire with the 60mm mortar; it could fire 3lb. high explosive and illuminating rounds out to ranges between 100 yards and just under 2,000 yards. Note the leather muzzle cap attached to the mortar's web sling.

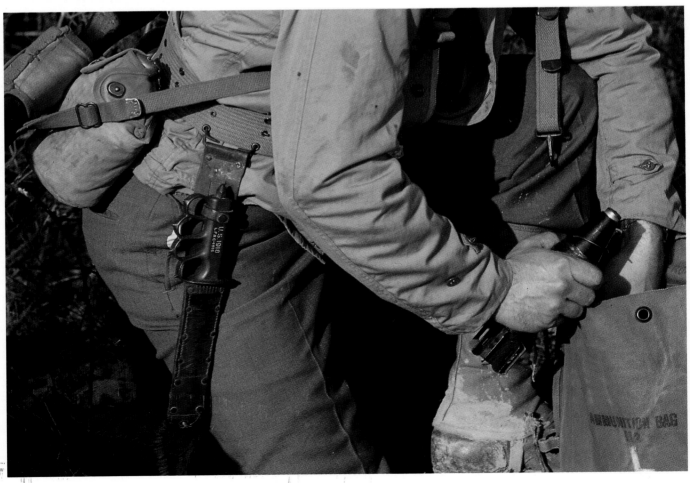

(Above) *An 81mm mortar squad make their way along a hedgerow. The sergeant in the lead carries a spade from the pioneer rack on the section's weapons carrier vehicle, to use when bedding in the mortar baseplate. The second soldier carries the M1 mortar barrel, the third has the baseplate and the fourth the bipod; he is followed by three ammunition carriers - a mortar in action eats up rounds at an enormous rate, and any spare soldier might find himself pressed into service as a "mule". Most are armed with pistols or M1 carbines, the lighter and handier alternative to the rifle which was popular, among those who could get them, as the personal weapon of soldiers who had other primary tasks. Most wear the light-weight gasmask case.*

(Left) *In the foreground, the baseplate for the 81mm mortar; the second man, wearing horsehide gloves, carries the bipod cushioned on a canvas shoulder pad. The total weight of the mortar's three components was 136lbs.*

(Above) Detail of the padded canvas load-carrying shoulder pads, issued in linked pairs, here used by the GI carrying the M1 81mm mortar tube. A battalion weapons company's mortar platoon had six one-tube squads organised in three two-squad sections. The 81mm mortar threw a variety of HE, illuminating and smoke rounds out to ranges between 100 and nearly 3,300 yards, by means of up to six charge increments for the bombs.

(Right) The M2 ammunition bag, slung poncho-fashion over the chest and back and strapped at the sides, was not solely used to carry mortar bombs; amongst other things it accomodated two boxes each with 250 rounds of .30 cal. machine gun ammunition both in the front and the back sections. It would take at least four rounds of 81mm in both front and back, and this soldier also lugs another four rounds in a wooden crate. The mortar can use up his entire load in one minute of rapid fire.

(Top left) While his buddies prepare their K-rations over an M1941 single burner gasoline stove, a GI unloads cardboard tubes with ammunition for the 4.2in. chemical mortar. The 4.2in. - the heaviest mortar normally found with line units - was not on the inventory of infantry units; intended for laying down major smoke or gas barrages, it was used by the Chemical Warfare Service in independent mortar battalions, which were then assigned to support infantry as needed. Since both sides avoided using toxic gas for fear of the consequences, the CW mortar battalions were given a more conventional support role with HE ammunition. With a range of some 5,000 yards they were a very valuable "pocket artillery" asset for the infantry commander.

(Bottom left) A GI reads the manual for the model SCR-625 mine detector; though not a weapon, it certainly saved a lot of GIs' lives. He wears an issue sleeveless sweater dated 11 October 1941.

Foot soldiers feared and hated mines; more often than not they only knew they were in a minefield when it was too late. The traditional infantry method of finding a safe path by crawling forward, probing gently in the earth with a bayonet, did not disappear with the issue of electro-magnetic detectors. These and their trained operators might be available on an important axis of advance in a major operation, but under most battlefield circumstances the GI still had to do it the hard way. Mines were laid in huge numbers in defensive warfare, and the Germans had a range of frighteningly effective anti-personnel types: mines which fired a steel rod upwards into the groin, mines which neatly clipped off half a foot, mines which jumped into the air before exploding at waist height in a murderous scythe of shrapnel.... In the Hurtgen Forest fighting in winter 1944-45 one stretch of track was found to have a mine planted every eight paces for three miles.

(Above) Two mine detector operators sweep a trackway. When these engineer specialists detect a contact they will mark it and move on, leaving it to the follow-up party to defuse and lift the mines. Both these types of detector were used at the front, but the SCR-625, at right, was more commonly seen than the later AN/PRS-1. Note the speaker for the SCR-625 mounted on the sling where it passes over the operator's left shoulder; and the power pack for the AN/PRS-1.

(Right) The harness for the AN/PRS-1 detector's power pack; one cable passes from the power pack to the detector handle, the other to the earphone yoke - here pulled down round the operator's neck.

Airborne Combat Dress

Though the idea of dropping heavily armed troops from aircraft behind enemy lines was first seriously proposed by Colonel Billy Mitchell in October 1918, and though experimental programs were mounted during the 1930s by the USSR, Germany, France and Italy, the Unites States forces did not pursue the idea until, in spring 1940, they were treated to the spectacle of Luftwaffe paratroop and glider units seizing vital positions in the defenses of Holland and Belgium for the following German motorised divisions.

This worrying demonstration resulted in the formation of the US Army's first parachute test platoon on 1 July 1940 at Fort Benning; this comprised 48 men selected from volunteers of the 29th Infantry Regiment, who made their first mass jump on the 29th of the same month. From these modest beginnings sprang the elite of the US Army, the Airborne (this title covering not only paratroopers but also air-landing glider units). The first full unit activated (on 1 October 1940) was the 501st Parachute Battalion. The 82nd and 101st Airborne Divisions were

activated, on paper, on 15 August 1942.

In November 1942 the 2/509th Parachute Infantry Regiment made the first combat jump during Operation "Torch" in French North Africa. In July 1943 elements of the 82nd Airborne Division and the 2/509th PIR took part in Operation "Husky", the invasion of Sicily. Both operations were costly failures; but hard lessons were learnt. By the eve of the Normandy landings in June 1944 the 82nd, by now veterans of hard fighting on the Italian mainland, and the unblooded 101st were both in England, poised to play a major part in the first battles for the liberation of Europe. In the pre-dawn darkness of 6 June 1944 they were among the very first Allied troops to set foot in German-occupied France; and in the weeks which followed they covered themselves with glory, though at a heavy cost in casualties.

(Left) Two paratroopers of the 82nd Airborne Division, England, summer 1944. Both wear the M1942 parachute jumper's coat and trousers, whose design - like that of the jump wings badge - is attributed to Captain William P. Yarborough, in 1941 the S2 of the Provisional Parachute Group. Of light-weight unlined cotton in a pale tan shade, the coat had a zipped front fly closure; four large bellows-type expanding patch pockets with slanted snap-fastened flaps, the upper pockets themselves slanted for easy of access when wearing equipment; snap fasteners at throat and cuff; and an integral cloth belt. The trousers had large expanding cargo pockets on each thigh. One trooper wears the M1C helmet with web A-straps and leather chin cup; the other his garrison cap, with the white and blue variant of the combined parachute/glider infantry badge (see page 13), and on his left shoulder the SSI of the 82nd ("All American") Airborne Division incorporating the "Airborne" tab. Note, left, the small USAAF issue ammunition pouch on the pistol belt. Next to this hangs an M1943 entrenching tool.

(Above) Rear view of the M1942 parachute jumper's uniform. On the left, note the bi-swing pleats in the back, and the expanding pleat in the center of the jacket back and skirt, between which the belt is sewn in place under the belt loop. The national flag patch was worn on the right arm by US Airborne units in all operations in the MTO and ETO: they were by definition spearhead troops, who risked confusing encounters. The GI on the right wears the M1936 pistol belt and suspenders; flanking an M1924 first aid pouch are an M1910 entrenching tool, an M1910 canteen, and the assault gasmask - intended only for short-term use - in its waterproof container. A wrist compass is strapped to his upper arm.

The M1942 uniform gave little protection from bad weather, and was often worn over OD wool clothing. It is often seen with reinforcement patches sewn to hard-wearing areas like the knees and elbows, sometimes in contrasting OD material.

(Left & below) Details of the M1C paratrooper's helmet. In 1942 the liner and chinstraps of the M1 were modified to absorb the shock of the parachute opening. The liner acquired two web A-straps, to the bottom of which buckled a leather chin cup; and to the web chinstrap of the helmet shell was added a short internal extension securing the shell to the liner by means of a snap fastener. The special Airborne first aid pack taped to the helmet net contains a field dressing, a tourniquet and a syrette of morphine.

Just visible (left) in the edge of the upper left coat closure is the small pocket, zipped on both sides for easy access with either hand, holding the M2 pocket knife; note the knife lanyard from this pocket to the right epaulette.

(Page 113 top left) The para-trooper's M2 pocket knife. This opened with a switchblade action, so that it could be used single-handed should he need to cut himself free from tangled shroud lines in case of an unlucky landing.

(Page 113 top right) The para-trooper, obliged to carry on his person everything needed for independent fighting and survival for several days in case relief forces were delayed, was normally festooned like a Christmas tree. On this M1936 pistol belt are a skein of rope, a lineman's leather pouch containing a pair of side-cutters and a folding knife, an M1911A1 pistol in its M1916 russet leather holster and, at the back, an M1910 T-handle entrenching tool.

(Page 113 bottom) On this pistol belt are a pair of the small but capacious USAAF-issue am-munition pouches favoured by paratroopers for their M1 carbine magazines. The GI is slipping his M3 fighting knife into the M8 scabbard strapped to his lower leg; note the unlined horsehide riding gloves, a popular and practical acquisition.

(Left) The inside surface and harness of the paratrooper's T-5 main parachute pack. This was the first US parachute to be specifically designed for paratroopers, and was in use from 1941 to 1945. A 28ft. canopy was attached by 28 shroud lines to a harness basically of the classic Irvin design, in which the lift webs attached to the shroud lines form a U-shape with a seat strap in which the paratrooper can (theoretically) sit, with extra straps round chest and thighs holding him in place, and three fastening points - strong metal snap hooks and D-rings at the chest and above each hip.

(Below) "Saddling up" needed co-operation from at least one other man, here boosting the T-5 pack up while the paratrooper slips his arms through the shoulder straps and takes the weight. The harness shoulder straps passing up each side of the body are overlaid by and buckled to the lift webs at the shoulder, the latter passing into the top of the parachute pack.

(Above) The leg straps are pulled through and up each side of the crotch to be secured above the hips. For over-water operations the B-4 aircrew life vest was standard issue; but in the event of the trooper landing in water he had to get rid of the parachute harness before inflating the vest, otherwise it would crush his chest. This was not an encouraging prospect given the layers of gear hampering his access to the three snap hook fastenings at chest and hips; near the end of the war some American parachutes were modified by the addition of a British quick-release box on the chest, which freed all the main attachments by a single twist and blow of the fist. In practice, loaded paratroopers who were unlucky enough to land in any but the shallowest water had virtually no chance of escaping drowning. A high proportion of parachuting injuries were also suffered when men were dragged across the drop zone by high winds, unable to release their harness.

(Right) Stowing the Thompson M1 sub-machine gun under the broad waist web of the T-5 harness. Note the M1908 Keer sling fitted to the Thompson.

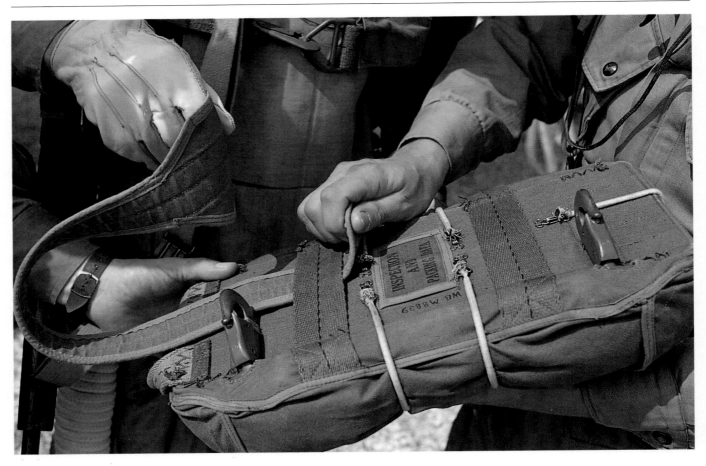

(Above) Attaching the chest pack reserve 'chute to the main harness. The waist web is passed through loops on the rear face of the pack and buckled tight on the left side of the body, and the two snap hooks are engaged with D-rings on the front of the harness shoulder straps. The US paratrooper, unlike his British comrade, had a reserve 'chute from the earliest days - it was not until the 1950s that the British paras followed suit. There are arguments for and against: having a reserve was no doubt good for morale, and may have saved a number of lives in training accidents. On the other hand, combat jumps were made from between 500 and 350ft., giving virtually no time to open a reserve if the main canopy failed, so the weight penalty was probably not worth it.

(Left & right) A US paratrooper ready to emplane for a 1944 training jump, burdened with both main and reserve 'chutes - note the red ripcord handle on the latter, which was manually operated; a life vest; his Thompson M1 sub-machine gun; his pack - the M1936 musette bag - slung below the reserve in front of his thighs; on his right hip the slung ammunition bag for Thompson or M3 "grease gun" magazines; and, under the parachute harness, his full web equipment with loaded pouches, canteen, pistol, entrenching tool, gasmask, rope skein, and other small equipment - visible are his fighting knife, and a TL122C angle-headed flashlight. For a combat jump this tech.5 would also have his suit pockets stuffed with as many extra magazines, grenades, K-rations and field dressings as they could accomodate. He is not, in fact, as heavily loaded as he might be.

Note here a variant of the helmet chin cup moulded with a more dished shape and a rim.

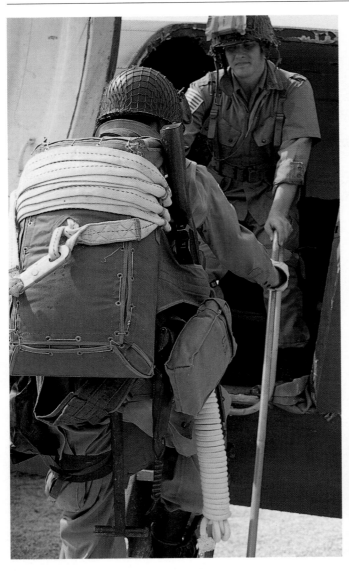

(Below) How to get rifles and light automatics safely onto the drop zone was a problem for all paratroopers. The British used a padded valise attached by a 20ft. rope to the parachute harness, and by two quick-release straps to the man's neck and leg. Once his 'chute deployed he pulled the quick-release cord, and paid out the rope so that the valise hit the ground before he did.

The US paratrooper used the similar "Griswold bag" carried by this GI, but did not lower it. It was attached to the harness by a short length of web and a snap hook on its rear face, and is here also taped to the leg for ease of movement. Before he jumps the trooper will untape it, holding it to his side as he goes out the door; the (relatively) slow landing speed of the T-5 should allow him to roll over it safely as he hits the dirt.

(Right) The 82nd Division paratrooper in the full equipment described in previous captions. Note also the wrist compass which he has strapped to his harness shoulder strap; the flat brown-painted can on his left ankle, which is a Hawkins mine; and the large padded canvas bag in his hand, which holds an AN/PPN-2 transmitter/receiver beacon.

A last word on the incredible loads carried by D-Day paratroopers comes from a private of the 101st Division: "...One suit of OD worn under my jump suit...main chute, reserve chute, Mae West, rifle, .45 automatic pistol, trench knife, jump knife, hunting knife, machete, one cartridge belt, two bandoliers, two cans of machine gun ammo totalling 676 rounds ...66 rounds of .45 ammo, one Hawkins mine capable of blowing the track off a tank, four blocks of TNT, one entrenching tool with two blasting caps taped on...three first aid kits, two morphine needles, one gasmask, one canteen of water, three days' supply of K-rations, two days' supply of D-rations...six fragment-ation grenades, one Gammon grenade, one orange smoke and one red smoke grenade, one orange panel, one blanket, one raincoat, one change of socks and underwear, two cartons of cigarettes, and a few other odds and ends..."

(Above) The paratrooper being helped aboard a C-47 Skytrain - when fully laden it was an achievement simply to stand up and walk. The C-47, the military version of the pre-war Douglas DC-3 commercial transport, formed the backbone of the Allied airlift fleet from 1942 onwards. This superbly reliable and versatile twin-engined aircraft could accomodate 20 fully equipped paratroopers, and could drop them at speeds between 85 and 100mph, so the slipstream was no problem.

In this view the pack of the T-5 main parachute is clearly seen. The web static line which operates it is coiled carefully across the back, held by elastics; the big metal snap hook, temporarily attached here, will be hooked up to a cable running along the cabin shortly before jumping. When the trooper leaves the door the static line pays out to its full length, then pulls out the rear panel of the pack by snapping the thin cord which is seen here lacing it in place round the edges. The rear panel is attached to the apex of the

'chute canopy by a breakable cord, which pulls it free of the pack before snapping. The canopy opens, pulling out the shroud lines after it.

These "canopy first" parachutes (in contrast to e.g. the British X-type, which deployed the shrouds before finally pulling the canopy out of an inner bag) gave a harder opening shock; but their faster deployment made them safer at low altitude. At Noemfoor, New Guinea, in July 1944 a paratroop force was mistakenly dropped from only 175ft., and apart from those unfortunates who hit 150ft. high trees, the battalion suffered surprisingly light casualties.

Readers who have only seen modern sports parachutists making "stand-up" landings with their light-weight, highly controllable rigs can have little idea of the landing shock felt by a fully loaded military parachutist of the 1940s. Commanders allowed for consider-able numbers of drop zone injury casualties on every combat jump, as an inevitable price to pay.

(Left & below) Studying the maps of the D-Day drop zones to check their position in the early morning light of 6 June 1944, these Pathfinders from the 101st Airborne Division use a light hand-held flare discharger as a paperweight. It is of interest to note that the maps used in this picture are the actual ones issued to the paratroopers for D-Day, showing "Omaha", "Utah" and the Normandy coastline.

The original 1942 organisation gave the Airborne Division 8,400 men — about half an Infantry Division's strength. By 1944 the 101st Airborne Division had been augmented: its major units were three Parachute Infantry Regiments each of three battalions (501st, 502nd & 506th PIRs), the two-battalion 327th Glider Infantry Regiment and one battalion of the 327th GIR, plus one Parachute and two Glider Field Artillery Battalions (377th PFAB, 321st & 907th GFABs).

Known as the "Screaming Eagles" from their shoulder patch, the 101st arrived in England in September 1943 and promptly began training for the invasion. On one night exercise they found their planes mixed in with a Luftwaffe bombing raid; jumping out into the flak-torn night sky, the GIs were mistaken for German paratroopers by the British Home Guard, and it took most of the next day for their officers to recover them from lock-ups around the south of England.

The 101st made their very first combat jump in the pre-dawn darkness over Normandy on D-Day. Their DZs were north of Carentan; their mission, to seize and hold vital routes inland through swampy country behind "Utah" beach. Severely scattered by heavy enemy flak, only about 2,500 men of the 101st managed to link up into viable units; they were dispersed over miles of strange terrain, without much of their equipment. Despite this they seized most of their objectives, and linked up with the 4th Infantry Division at around noon on 6 June.

(Below) The aerial delivery bag Type A-5. These large padded canvas containers were used to parachute all kinds of munitions, heavy weapons and equipment, such as machine guns, mortars, radios, and even - broken down into several loads - the Parachute Artillery Regiments' 75mm pack howitzers. Note, left, the leg of the M1942 parachute jumper's trousers with sewn-in tapes brought around the leg and tied off, to help support the weight of heavily loaded cargo pockets.

(Right) A Pathfinder from 101st Airborne Division sets up an AN/PPN-2 transmitter/receiver beacon. The padded bag to the right is its carrier. In the background another GI is setting out bright yellow and cerise colored silk air-recognition panels, used to signal to aircraft.

The Pathfinders of the 101st are believed to have been the first Allied troops to actually set foot in France, landing at 12.15am on 6 June. After orienting themselves they set out flares as an aiming point for the following waves of C-47s. Sadly, the pilots of many of the transports were confused by a low cloud bank, and by very heavy enemy anti-aircraft fire. Some dropped their sticks too low, and others over the sea, with tragic consequences.

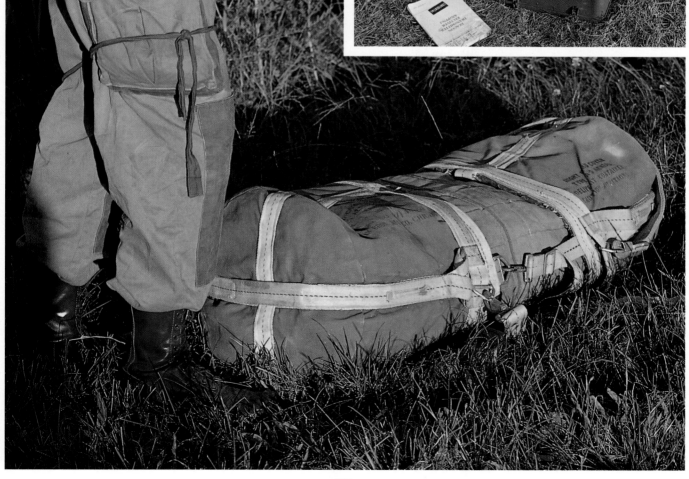

(Above) On the D-Day drop, US paratroopers improvised face camouflage from a mixture of linseed oil and cocoa powder. Note the lining of the leather chin cup of the M1C pattern helmet.

(Left) Detail of the special cut-down model M1928 entrenching tool carried by the paratroopers of the 505th and 2/509th PIRs in North Africa in 1943, together with the 16in. M1942 bayonet. Note that, like all the early paratroopers, this GI has the M1918 mounted cartridge belt with the pistol ammunition pocket.

(Right) A technician/grade 3 of the 101st Airborne Division sets up a folding litter; the hinges show in the canvas cut-outs in the middle of the poles. The markings date it from 1942. These folding litters were not specifically Airborne issue equipment. Note, again, the Hawkins mine strapped to the paratrooper's left ankle; this was one of a number of devices issued to the Airborne in an attempt to make up for their lack of heavy weapons - another was the Gammon grenade - which were (theoretically) capable of at least immobilising enemy tanks. While technically sound, all these basically hand-delivered devices demanded nerve, skill and luck.

After Normandy, the 82nd and 101st next saw action in Holland on 17 September 1944 in Operation "Market Garden", the largest airborne assault in history. Despite heroic fighting this Allied attempt to seize a corridor for ground troops into the Ruhr via the bridges at Eindhoven, Nijmegen and Arnhem was ultimately a failure.

(Above) Preparing their gear, perhaps for one of the many operations which were planned but then cancelled during summer and early fall 1944, these paratroopers all wear the M1943 field jacket and trousers; the drive to standardise combat clothing saw the M1942 suit (criticised for its conspicuous color, and lack of warmth) largely withdrawn after the Normandy campaign. The man at left has a slung M1A1 folding-stock carbine. The center soldier holds a Browning .30 cal. machine gun tripod; he kneels beside one of the paratrooper "leg bags" acquired from the British Army, which took various weapon and equipment loads up to at least 80lbs. weight. It was attached to the paratrooper for the jump by quick-release straps; he pulled the pins from these as soon as his canopy deployed, slowly paying out the attached 15ft. rope by means of a canvas grip. The bag hit the ground long enough before he did for his canopy to give him full support at impact. The GI kneeling on the right, stowing an SCR-536 radio, has attached to his webbing the special canvas holster for the M1A1 folding-stock carbine, and just behind it can be seen a dark green webbing demolition bag for carrying 1/2lb. TNT charges.

(Left) Airborne officer, fall 1944, wearing M1943 jacket, M1943 trousers with added cargo pockets, M1C helmet, and 1943 issue OD shade 7 web equipment. On his belt he has an M1942 first aid pouch and M1938 wire cutters; his .45 pistol is carried in an M3 shoulder holster. His gloves are private purchase. Although an officer, note that he wears no collar insignia of rank in the field - a quite common practice. The national flag recognition symbol is worn here in brassard form.

(Left) The officer packs an airborne medic's bag. His folding-stock carbine was not nearly as widely issued to Airborne troops as is popularly supposed. Originally it was only authorised issue to the Engineer Battalion in an Airborne Division; although it was acquired by men of other units it never became general issue to the infantry - its round lacked the stopping power of the rifle and sub-machine gun, and it should be seen as a "pistol replacement" rather than as a main infantry weapon.

At right, note again the British leg bag; the lowering rope and its web grip can be seen stowed in an outer tube of canvas. Controlling the rate of lowering by angling the canvas grip was a tricky but vital technique: a runaway bag could tear right off the harness, and inflict fatal injuries on paratroopers below, either by collapsing their canopies in midair or simply by crushing them on the DZ.

(Below) Detail of the triple-compartment US Airborne medic's bag.

(Left) This paratrooper is stowing the tripod for the M1919 Browning .30 cal. air-cooled machine gun ready for packing in the British-made M1944 drop bag.

(Below) The Airborne troops' M3A4 utility handcart, loaded with .30 cal. ammunition cases and ready for stowing on a glider; the cart had a lace-on canvas cover.

(Right, top & bottom) The SCR-536/BC-611 "handie-talkie" radio, with its telescopic aerial closed down and covered with a screw-on protective cap, is zipped into its padded canvas bag for the drop. Note also detail of the wrist compass, the carbine holster, and the strong metal snap hook on the demolition bag.

(Above) A Pathfinder laying out some of his kit for checking before an operation. In front of him is a padded Griswold bag, on which lies an M1 rifle broken down into two parts ready for zipping into the bag. Under the paratrooper's knee is another Griswold bag, zipped up. Just visible under his left hand are three Hawkins mines, and above them three MkIIA1 fragmentation grenades. Notice the USAAF issue ammunition pouches on his M1936 pistol belt. He is holding one of the luminous discs which the Pathfinders attached to the back of their helmets as a night location aid. In the center is the AN/PPN-2 radio beacon; on the right, the T-5 parachute main and reserve packs, a demolition bag, and the M1936 field (musette) bag.

(Left) Close-up of a Pathfinder's luminous helmet disc.

(Top right) Tools of the trade: a paratrooper checking the load in the magazine of a Thompson .45 cal. M1 sub-machine gun...

(Right) ...and a close-up of the M3 fighting knife, strapped to a paratrooper's leg in an M8 plastic scabbard. The canvas is an opened-out Griswold bag on which he is field-stripping a Colt .45 cal. M1911A1 pistol. Note that he wears the M1943 combat boots, with reverse uppers, rather than "Corcoran" jump boots; as with the M1943 field uniform, these general issue boots became common among Airborne troops late in the war (to the consternation of veterans, both for reasons of pride and because it was feared that the buckled straps might foul shroud lines during a jump).

(Right & below) Two paratroopers of the 101st Airborne Division saddling up for their jump over Zon on the Wilhelmina Canal during Operation "Market Garden" on 17 September 1944. The GI on the right has an M1 bayonet and an early M1924 first aid pouch on his cartridge belt. Note the white "ace of spades" painted on his helmet under the netting, the tactical symbol of the 506th PIR; the Division's 501st PIR used a diamond, the 502nd a heart. Both men wear the M1943 jacket and trousers; the modification to the trousers is clearly seen on the left - the added cargo pockets are a noticeably different color from the trousers. Despite its size the individual weapons bag was sometimes worn under the harness, behind the reserve 'chute; one imagines this must have caused breathing problems, especially at the moment the canopy opened.

(Top right) Wesel, Germany, March 1945: after the Rhine crossing jump a paratrooper of the 17th Airborne Division uses the SCR-536 radio, its open carrier slung on his chest. Note the later style web strap chin cradle on the helmet at left.

(Right) An Airborne medic attends a paratrooper with a twisted ankle; note the special medical bag on his back.

(Above) Paratroopers of the 17th Airborne hurry across open ground. They all wear M1943 jackets and modified M1943 trousers, and M1943 combat boots. Webbing includes rifle cartridge and pistol belts, M1936 suspenders and field bags, and light-weight gasmask cases. The two GIs on the left are a bazooka team; the two at right rear are pulling an M4A3 utility cart loaded with ammunition. Note the bright yellow scarves made from British-issue individual air identification panels of truncated triangle shape.

(Right) A bazooka team from 17th Airborne wait in hiding. Note the empty holster for an M1A1 folding-stock carbine hooked to the Number 1's belt and strapped round his lower leg.

(Opposite top) Interestingly, as well as a scarf made from a British silk ID panel, this paratrooper wears British-made web equipment: note the British buckles on the suspenders, and the much coarser weave than in US webbing.

(Opposite bottom) A paratrooper fires his M1A1 carbine from cover - the ejected shell can just be seen above the breech. Under his arm is slung a demolition bag. The strap on his left wrist is a compass.

Armored Combat Dress

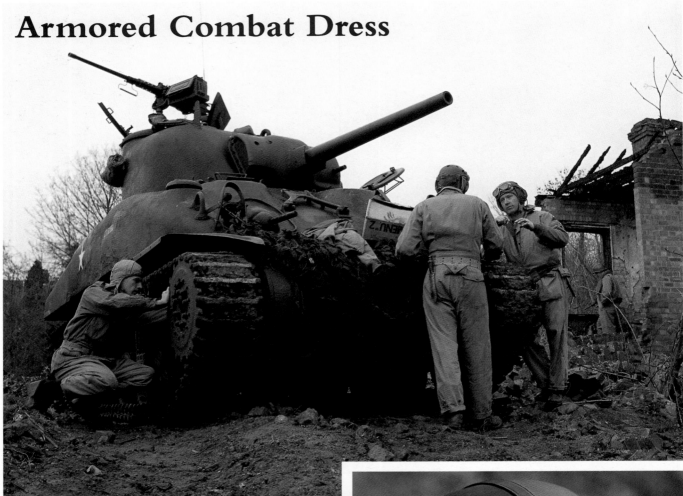

(Above) *Germany, 1945: a pause in the grinding advance gives the crew of an M4A1 Sherman tank a chance to "unbutton" the hatches and come up for air.*

(Right) *Detail of the M1942 armored forces helmet. Designed to protect the wearer from the many sharp protrusions inside the lurching tank turret and hull, it gave no ballistic protection. Attached to the green-painted hard leather skull piece are a riveted neck guard and two cheek pieces; the lining was tan leather. The earphones are mounted in the cheek pieces, which are held to the head by two flat, leather-covered metal springs mounted on swivels above the rim of the skull piece. Snap-fastened leather straps or elastic strips connected the neck guard to the cheek pieces and also held goggle straps and headphone leads in place. Just visible under the helmet are the chin strap and neck piece of the padded winter combat helmet. Points of interest are the US-made goggles with the Canadian War Department cypher, and a 2nd Armored Division patch, mounted on OD felt, which was made in Britain.*

(Opposite) *The crewman on the right wears the rank of a technician/grade 3 and his divisional patch on his winter combat jacket. Early versions of this jacket had patch pockets, instead of the slash pockets shown here. Both versions had the OD knit collar, waist band and elasticated cuffs and the full-length front zipper. Note the difference between the US-made M1942 first aid pouch on the left and the M1924 pattern on the right. The trench knife on the left hand man's belt is the M3 in the leather M6 scabbard. Note the bi-swing back and single buttoned, flapped rear pocket of his second pattern one-piece HBT suit, and also the two metal buttons under the collar for attaching a hood.*

(Above & left) Good views of the ventilation holes in the top of the tanker's helmet, and its leather lining. The commander's goggles are dated 1938 and marked "Resistol". Note the square-cornered knit collar of the jacket (dated 10 February 1941); and details of the commander's M1938 despatch case. Behind him is the pintle-mounted M2 Browning .50 cal. heavy machine gun.

(Above right) The winter combat jacket was made of windproof and water repellent cotton lined throughout with OD blanket (kersey) material. It was extremely popular with all GIs, not just tankers; and many a "dogface" would haggle with armored crews to get one. Here an infantry sergeant, left, wearing the OD field jacket, light OD wool trousers, a woollen scarf and the M1941 knit cap, is trading serious front line currency with a 6th Armored Division staff sergeant, who is still in possession of his bib-fronted winter combat trousers - note zip access to the

pocket of any trousers worn underneath.

(Right & far right) Rear and front views of the winter combat trousers very frequently worn by tank crews in cold weather. Made of windproof and water repellent tan cotton with full blanket lining, they have a central zipped closure from the top of the bib to the crotch. The first pattern had the suspenders permanently sewn down at both ends, a zipped access in the right side seam only, and ties at the outside ankle vents. The second pattern, illustrated, had metal buttons and clips at the front ends of the suspenders, zipped access through both side seams, a small zipped access for toilet purposes (just visible here on the front of the left thigh), and snap-fastened tabs at the outside ankle vents.

Note also his M1944 single-lens goggles; and the plastic buttons on the HBT jacket - these began to appear on both one- and two-piece HBT suits in mid-1944.

(Above) Both crewmen wear the second pattern HBT one-piece suit - note tongueless frame buckle of the integral belt, left - and the commander the winter combat helmet. Tank crew web equipment was typically limited to a pistol belt with a holstered .45, magazine pocket and first aid pouch.

(Right) The winter combat helmet recommended for wear alone or under the armored forces' helmet in cold weather. Designed to be worn with the flap tucked into the jacket collar, the helmet channelled rainwater straight into the seat of the wearer's pants....It is worn here with the M1944 Polaroid all-purpose goggles, which had interchangeable clear and tinted lenses.

(Opposite) A typical assortment of tanker's clothing worn by a crew evidently confident that they are far

from any threat. Sitting on the turret, the commander and gunner wear winter combat jackets over one-piece HBT suits. The loader, with his back to camera, is wearing the M1943 jacket and a winter combat helmet. The co-driver has winter combat trousers over an OD field jacket, wool scarf and M1941 knit cap; his tanker's helmet is in his left hand. The driver also wears the tanker's helmet and M1938 "Resistol" goggles.

(Overleaf, pages 140–141) Smoke break: can it all be over at last? Note here how the leads emerge from the back of the earphones and pass round to the front, where they terminate in a jack-plug which connects to the tank intercom system. The commander, left, has a modified M1916 holster for his .45 cal. pistol, with the flap cut away to leave only a strap to retain the pistol.